Spirit Car

spirit Car

Journey to a Dakota Past

DIANE WILSON

**BOREALIS
BOOKS**

Borealis Books is an imprint of the
Minnesota Historical Society Press.
www.borealisbooks.org

The Minnesota Historical Society Press is a member of
the Association of American University Presses.

Manufactured in the United States of America

10 9 8 7 6 5 4 3 2

∞ The paper used in this publication meets the mini-
mum requirements of the American National Standard for Information Sciences—Permanence for Printed
Library Materials, ANSI Z39.48–1984.

International Standard Book Number
ISBN-13: 978–0-87351–765-2 (paper)

Library of Congress Cataloging-in-Publication Data
Wilson, Diane
  Spirit car : journey to a Dakota past / Diane Wilson.
  p. cm.
Includes bibliographical references.
ISBN-13: 978-0-87351-570-2 (cloth : alk. paper)
ISBN-10: 0-87351-570-6 (cloth : alk. paper)
  1. Wilson, Diane.
  2. Dakota Indians—Biography.
  3. Dakota Indians—History.
  4. Dakota Indians—Government relations.
  I. Title.

E99.D1W84 2006
978.004'975243—dc22   2006009894

The lines from Pauline Danforth's "For My Grandmothers" on page 3 are reprinted with permission of
Pauline Danforth. Photographs on pages 8, 43, and
194 are from the collections of the Minnesota Historical Society; the photograph on page 199 was provided
by Waziyatawin Angela Wilson; all other images are
from the author's collections.

For Lucille

Spirit Car

Author's Note

This book contains a variety of material: stories, facts, speculation, and insights. The stories in Book One are based on real people whose lives have been reimagined on a bedrock of facts. I wanted to bring the facts alive, to see and feel history transformed into a living, breathing reality with human beings who cared deeply about their families, about their lives. My family's stories of the 1862 Dakota War, for example, have been lost, but a great deal of information exists about the war and its aftermath. Using a technique that writer LeAnne Howe once described as "intuitive anthropology," writers can extrapolate stories from the historical record. I used extensive research to make these stories as historically accurate as possible, while I tried to imagine how it would feel, for example, to take refuge at Fort Ridgely in 1862. In a sense, these are ghost stories, written to re-create a family history that has been lost over time, or repressed as too painful, or simply set aside as the gritty issues of survival demanded attention. Re-creating certain moments in history and reliving them through my own imagination has allowed me to know earlier generations of my family as human beings.

Readers can trust the information in these stories as having come from solid, dependable sources: scholarship, historical research, interviews, and firsthand experience. The small details—eating fry bread after school, drinking goat's milk—came from interviews or research. The letters quoted are real, all of the people existed, and I visited each place that I wrote about. I imagined conversations and feelings based on plausible assumptions and the intuitive understanding I gained of these people after burrowing inside their lives.

Book Two continues the narrative with stories from my life, especially those drawn from the long search to understand my family's Dakota identity. My intent was to write a memoir in which I serve as a guide through a larger story. The further I dug into the past, the harder I was pulled to create a narrative that would make sense of my family's history, beginning in 1862. The result: an historical or family memoir that combines a bit of everything in telling a story that spans five generations. In the process, I discovered just how deeply our identities are influenced by the forces of history.

For a more detailed explanation of the sources of information used in each chapter, see the Source Notes section at the end of the book. In the text, there is a shift in tribal name from Sioux to Dakota. In contemporary writing, the term "Sioux" has generally been replaced with "Dakota," but "Sioux" was the tribal name often used in the 1800s, especially in government documents. As much as possible, I have used "Dakota" to indicate the people known as the *Oceti Sakowin* or Seven Council Fires, which includes the Santee Sioux or Dakota in the east (the Mdewakanton, Wahpekute, Sisseton, and Wahpeton in Minnesota, in South Dakota, and at Santee, Nebraska), the Nakota in the middle (the Yankton and Yanktonais, in South Dakota), and the Lakota in the west (the Tetons, in North and South Dakota).

spirit Car

BOOK ONE

Grandmothers, complainers and nags,
they poke at me and tug my sleeve.
'Listen to us granddaughter,
our voices are real, these things did happen.
Our time has gone by, but our pain lingers on.
Tell our stories, learn from our lives.
Keep our words with you, don't let our ways die.'

PAULINE BRUNETTE DANFORTH
"For My Grandmothers"

1 *Step Back in Time*

NOVEMBER 6, 2002
Lower Sioux Reservation, Minnesota

The motel clock on my bedside table read 4:10 AM, too early to get up and too late to hope for more sleep. I lay still with my eyes closed, trying to recall the dream that woke me and left a feeling of anxious violence lingering in its wake. I threw back the covers, then pushed open the drapes so that I could at least see the prairie night sky and a few stars beyond the casino's bright lights.

My overnight bag sat on the luggage stand, neatly packed and ready for an early departure. I had left my notebooks on the table, along with a few reference books, to be packed quickly in the morning. My books detailed the history of the Lower Sioux reservation where I was staying at the Jackpot Junction Casino in Morton, Minnesota, about three hours southwest of Minneapolis. Before falling asleep I reread the chapter on the 1862 Dakota War, a bloody conflict between the Dakota and white settlers that had been fought in this area. Those were the images that haunted my dreams.

In the morning, just before sunrise, I would meet my younger brother Dave in the motel lobby. He told me later that he could not sleep, that he too woke just after 4:00 AM. Sitting on the edge of his bed, he spent the rest of the night quietly plucking at his guitar.

I wondered how many other rooms were filled with people like us, who had come to be part of the first-ever Dakota Commemorative March. This event was planned to honor the Dakota who had been forced to walk 150 miles from the Lower Sioux reservation to a prison camp at Fort Snelling after the 1862 war.

We were supposed to meet before daybreak at St. Cornelia's Church, not far from the casino motel, beginning the walk shortly after dawn. The group planned to walk more than twenty miles each day, regardless of weather, arriving at Fort Snelling the following week. The March would follow roughly the same route as the original, commemorating the 140th anniversary of a painful history that had never before been publicly acknowledged.

I had invited my brother to join me, but I had not known whether Dave would actually come until I spotted his car in the parking lot. I felt immense relief. Neither of us knew anyone who was involved in planning or participating in this event. We checked in, then went in search of the group, which was gathering somewhere in Morton for an evening meal and a sweat lodge ceremony. Although the town of Morton is only a few blocks long, we could not find anyone who knew anything about the March. Confused and uncertain, we agreed to stay the night. If the next morning did not go well, we would find a way to leave early in the day.

Eleven years of retracing our family history had led me here to the March, but this long journey began with my mother, Lucille Dion Wilson. She was enrolled on the Rosebud reservation in South Dakota, where she grew up. Between the ages of ten and sixteen, she attended the Holy Rosary Mission School, a boarding school on the Pine Ridge reservation. After moving to Minneapolis, she eloped with Chuck Wilson, a tall Swede from central Minnesota, and raised five children in a white suburb. When I was growing up, she told me that she was done with "all that," referring to her Indian heritage. "We were poor," she said. "I'm glad to be out of it." With a stubborn lift of her chin, she then refused to say more. Her reluctance to speak about her past, the silence that surrounded her years at boarding school, seemed impenetrable.

At that time, I had no idea why boarding schools existed, nor any sense of the history that surrounded the reservation system. Reading the word "assimilation" in my history book at school inspired the same yawn-inducing, this-is-dry-as-dirt reaction that I felt reading about history in general. Manifest Destiny, Lewis and

Clark, the 1862 Dakota War meant nothing to me. Those events had all happened a long time ago to other people and had no relevance to my life.

My mother, on the other hand, was a mystery. All of us kids kept asking questions, trying to squeeze out whatever information we could get any time we were alone with her. Her life, her unimaginable life, dangled before us like a long thread reaching to the past, the single unraveled edge of something that was much larger than we could even begin to guess.

One afternoon, my mother told me about being left for two years at the boarding school until her family could afford to send for her. She would repeat the story to my sister and my brothers, one at a time, without blame or bitterness, as if to make a point, to teach a lesson. But she did not say, in the usual way she and her sisters liked to end a story about a difficult time in their lives, "We made the best of it." There was an undercurrent of emotion that she had never acknowledged except in telling this one story. For years afterward, her words flashed their weak signal to me like a firefly in the bushes. I knew that one day I would need to learn what they hid.

In my thirties, I began retracing my family's trail across South Dakota and Nebraska, where I gathered facts, anecdotes, and sepia-tinted photographs of relatives faded to a ghostlike image, and I second-guessed history when the information dried up. The struggle to understand the gap between my mother's past and my life, and the leap she made from Pine Ridge to Golden Valley, led me to the 1862 war and the Lower Sioux reservation. What began as a simple question about my mother evolved into a search for understanding about culture and identity and family legacy.

At 5:00 AM I turned on the lamp and began to pack. The sun would not rise for at least another hour, and there was plenty of time before I would meet Dave in the lobby. On the desk lay the flyer that had come in the mail a month earlier, offering its scant details about the March. A line drawing from the June 1863 issue of *Harper's New Monthly Magazine* showed men and women from New Ulm attacking Dakota captives riding through town in a wagon. A shower of sticks and rocks fell on the Dakota, while white women in long dresses stood poised to hurl more, their faces focused in rage upon their victims.

I had been surprised that so much attention would be given to an event that was little more than a footnote in history books. Most of the accounts focused on the six-week war that exploded in August 1862 on the Lower Sioux reservation from the frustrations of failed treaties. Hundreds of white settlers were killed and their farms were destroyed. When the war was over, much of the white population of Minnesota demanded that the Dakota people be forcibly removed from the state, regardless of which side they had supported during the war. The march was usually mentioned briefly as a four-mile train of about 1,700 Dakota, mostly women, children, and elders, who were forced to walk under military guard through towns filled with outraged settlers to a prison camp near the Mississippi River at Fort Snelling.

I had stumbled into this history two years earlier while searching for information about my great-great-grandmother, Rosalie Marpiya Mase, or Iron Cloud, a full-blood Dakota woman. After years of chasing my family's story, the trail finally led me to Rosalie, who lived directly across the Minnesota River from the

Citizens of New Ulm attacking Dakota captives, in Harper's New Monthly Magazine, *June 1863*

Agency on the Lower Sioux reservation, where the war began. No one in my family knew much about Rosalie or her involvement in the war. I had only recently learned that when the fighting started, she and her French-Canadian husband, Louis LaCroix, had taken refuge at Fort Ridgely with the white settlers. Rosalie and her seven mixed-blood children were among the few Dakota who were not forced to march to Fort Snelling, who remained behind in Minnesota after the war.

Rosalie was the reason I had come to be part of the March. Although she was spared the traumatic experience of the march, she was involved in the violent war that had preceded it. My theory—which is how I understood history, by analyzing it—was that Rosalie's separation from her community was as harsh, in some ways, as that experienced by the people who were imprisoned at Fort Snelling. I was there because her survival had also come at a terrible cost.

What I did not know in those early morning hours was whether that tenuous connection to the March would be accepted by Dakota people whose families had lost everything, sometimes even their lives. I lay awake partly from the anxiety that comes from walking into a gathering of Indian people who are focused on remembering a violent and tragic part of the past. The Dakota War had inspired a deep hatred between whites and Indians, feelings that sometimes still lie just beneath the surface. My brother is dark like our mother, but I look like a middle-aged, middle-class, green-eyed *wasichu*.

My comfort, then, came from those notebooks and history books still stacked on my table. They were my only defense, my protection against the forces that had drawn me here. I knew the facts about the 1862 war well enough to dream them at night. I also had a car out in the parking lot with a full tank of gas, ready for flight in case the event proved unwelcoming or, worse, disorganized and a waste of time.

I reached for the fanny pack that I would wear while I walked. From the zippered pouch on the back, I pulled out a photo of my mother that was taken before she started chemotherapy. Smoothing a crease in the corner, I studied her smiling face and thought about our conversation the day before. She was curious about our presence at the March.

"I don't know why you kids are so interested in all that stuff," she said. In the background, I could hear my dad muttering, *Why don't they schedule this thing in warmer weather?* He couldn't imagine why anyone would willingly walk 150 miles in cold November weather for something that had happened so long ago. At the same time, he wanted to help even if he didn't understand. *Do you kids* (I was forty-seven, my brother forty-five) *need any money? Don't hesitate to call if you have trouble. May the good Lord* (Lutheran) *be with you.*

I could not explain to my mother why I was here, except that I had to come. Years earlier, I thought that understanding why she was left at boarding school was all that I needed. Somewhere in the desolate plains of South Dakota I had realized that wasn't enough; images had begun to fill my head, together with scraps of words.

I discovered a new truth: I was searching for the stories that had been lost from our family. In traditional Dakota culture, stories are handed down from one generation to the next. The loss of that oral tradition and the breakdown of communication between generations had set my family adrift, floating aimlessly without history and all its accumulated experience to guide us. As human beings we need our stories surrounding us. We need context, we need myths, we need family legends in order to see the invisible legacy that follows us, that tells us who we are.

Eleven years earlier I had begun my search with almost no knowledge of the past. I slowly gathered information that became grist for long-dormant stories that rebuilt a connection between the generations in my family. Each story carried me, unsuspecting, further back in time toward the 1862 Dakota War. This was the moment in history that reverberates through generations of family, an epochal event for Dakota people and the state of Minnesota, whose consequences continue to ripple through our lives.

The story begins on a warm day in 1862, when a long-denied rage was about to be unleashed as an act of war.

2 *Dakota War of 1862*

AUGUST 15, 1862
Lower Sioux Reservation, Minnesota

On a hill above the Minnesota River, a sultry breeze rustled the leaves of the tall trees that lined the riverbank. Not far from the Redwood or Lower Sioux Agency, a steep path wound down to the ferry landing where the boat sat idly waiting for its next passengers. On the other side, a dirt road led to Fort Ridgely, twelve miles to the east, past a handful of log cabins widely separated by fields and woods.

The Lower Sioux Agency, a collection of tidy government buildings that included a school, sawmill, and stone warehouse, was the center of the Lower Sioux reservation on the Minnesota River. This narrow strip of land was the new home for the Dakota people, who once hunted and lived throughout the southern half of Minnesota. The government had persuaded, manipulated, and threatened the Dakota until they finally signed the treaty of 1851, making way for thousands of acres of wild prairie to be plowed under for crops.

In exchange for payments of cash and goods, the Dakota agreed to leave their villages, their burial grounds, and their hunting fields and woods, and to give up their ability to move about the land as free men and women. Many of them lived in villages near the confluence of the Minnesota and Mississippi rivers, an area that is sacred to the Dakota.

As soon as the treaties were signed, white settlers flooded the ceded land, swarming across the Dakotas' fields, their homes, and their gardens long before they were prepared to move to the reservation.

11

By the summer of 1862, four bands of the eastern Dakota—Mdewakanton, Sisseton, Wahpeton, and Wahpekute—were living on the reservation. The Sisseton and Wahpeton settled around the Upper Sioux Agency, about thirty miles upstream near the mouth of the Yellow Medicine River, while the Mdewakanton and Wahpekute reluctantly left their villages to relocate on the river near the Redwood, or Lower Sioux, Agency.

When the first treaty payment arrived, the Dakota discovered they had been tricked into signing a paper that diverted much of their money into paying traders' debts. As their resentment at being confined to the reservation continued to grow, few promises were kept to build schools, and annuity goods carrying exorbitant prices often turned up for sale in traders' stores. Government officials failed to investigate traders' misconduct, ignoring illegal liquor sales and mistreatment of Dakota women by white men. Annuity payments, which were often late, became even less predictable as the Civil War grew longer and more costly.

It may have been the arrogance of the whites toward the Dakota, however, that cut the deepest. Chief Big Eagle said, "Many of the whites always seemed to say by their manner when they saw an Indian, 'I am much better than you,' and the Indians did not like this." The constant pressure to become farmers, give up their traditions, even their religion, was a source of great resentment toward whites.

On this warm day in mid-August, a crowd of angry Dakota men and women were waiting near the locked warehouse at the Lower Agency where the annuity goods were stored, while their children played in the long grass behind the traders' stores. They had been waiting for months for the cash, food, and goods that had been promised to them.

Suddenly they heard raised voices, angry words shouted by the men who were meeting nearby. The traders—Louis Robert, Andrew Myrick, François La Bathe, and others—sat together, leaving clerks in charge of their stores. Across from them Taoyateduta, also known as Little Crow, watched the Indian agent,

Thomas Galbraith, with an expression that was both stern and without hope. Several of his warriors stood on either side of him. Galbraith was refusing to honor his promise to issue more provisions—those belonging to the Dakota by treaty and already stockpiled in the warehouse—even though the Indians were starving. The annuity payment that was due at the end of June had not yet been received. After the near-failure of the previous year's crops, followed by a bitter winter, by the spring of 1862 many Dakota were living on roots and scarce game. The early distribution of a few provisions in June had kept the Dakota alive, but they were again desperate for the food that was locked away. Captain Marsh from Fort Ridgely had been called out earlier that month when they broke into the warehouse at the Upper Agency.

Galbraith, an arrogant and indecisive man, told Little Crow that he did not know when the annuity money was coming. It had always been his custom to distribute the food with the money, and he did not want to deviate from his prescribed routine.

Little Crow looked at Galbraith for a long moment. He said, through his interpreter, "We have waited a long time. The money is ours, but we cannot get it. We have no food, but here are these stores, filled with food. We ask that you, the agent, make some arrangement by which we can get food from the stores, or else we may take our own way to keep ourselves from starving. When men are hungry they help themselves."

Galbraith kept his eyes on the floor as Little Crow spoke. In the silence that followed, he rubbed his chin and appeared deep in thought. Finally, he turned toward the traders and spread his hands. "Well, sirs, you hear for yourselves the situation that Little Crow is in. Is there anything that you can do to help?" He was asking whether they would continue to extend credit to the Dakota for food.

With a show of reluctance, the traders turned to each other and spoke in low voices. Finally, Myrick threw his hands in the air and stood up, as if he were about to leave. "Sir," Galbraith called. "We are waiting on your decision."

Andrew Myrick turned back toward the group and addressed

Galbraith. "So far as I am concerned, if they are hungry, let them eat grass."

A long silence followed as Little Crow considered the interpreter's translation of these words. Finally, with a terrible whoop, he and his warriors left.

A few days after the disappointing meeting at the Lower Agency, four Wahpeton men were walking home from a hunting trip in the Big Woods of Kandiyohi, over thirty miles east of the Lower Agency. They were tired and hungry, with many miles yet to cover before they reached their encampment on the Minnesota River. The men were Sungigidan (Brown Wing), Ka-om-de-i-ye-dan (Breaking Up), Nagi-wi-cak-te (Killing Ghost), and Pa-zo-i-yo-pa (Runs Against Something When Crawling) from the Rice Creek band that had separated from Shakopee's village on the Redwood River.

They came to a fence surrounding land in Acton Township that belonged to Robinson Jones, a white man they knew who ran a post office and store. As they approached, a hen flew up and left her eggs hidden in the grass. One of the men bent to pick up the eggs, but his companion warned him not to touch them. "Don't take them, for they belong to a white man and we may get into trouble."

Instead of setting the eggs down, the man smashed them on the ground. Turning to his companion in a fury, he said, "You are a coward. You are afraid of the white man. You are afraid to take even an egg from him, though you are half-starved."

"I am not a coward," the other replied. "I am not afraid of the white man, and to show you that I am not I will go to the house and shoot him. Are you brave enough to go with me?"

"Yes, I will go with you, and we will see who is the braver of us two." All four men walked up to the house. Robinson Jones became alarmed and left his two children behind while he hurried to the home of Howard Baker, where his wife was visiting. The hunters followed him and challenged the whites to a target-shooting contest. Instead of shooting at the target, they turned without warning and shot Jones and his wife, Baker, and Viranus Webster, who was visiting the Bakers. When the Dakotas left, they passed the Jones place and shot fifteen-year-old Clara Wilson.

The men stole several horses and hurried back toward their village, realizing that there would be consequences but having little idea just how devastating they would be.

They rode hard to reach home by evening and wasted no time in finding their headman, Hochokaduta or Red Middle Voice, to tell him what they had done. He knew immediately that the men were in deep trouble that could affect their village and possibly the entire tribe. They had killed white women, and this violent act would surely bring the soldiers to punish them and possibly stop the annuity payment from arriving at all.

Red Middle Voice and his followers rode quickly to Shakopee's large village downstream, to the east. When they told the chief what had happened, his warriors declared their eagerness to make war on the whites, but Shakopee would not commit his people without the backing of the other Lower Sioux bands. They decided to convene a council of chiefs that same night at Little Crow's village. He alone had the prestige and experience they would need to lead the war. Riders were sent to summon Mankato, Wabasha, Wacouta, Traveling Hail, and Big Eagle to Little Crow's house, not far from the Lower Agency.

As Little Crow listened to the appeals of the young men for war, he blackened his face as a sign of mourning and covered his head. Several of the chiefs argued for peace, and the future of the Dakota people hung in the balance as they wrestled with the decision. The frustration that had been building over many years of broken treaty promises and the humiliating demand that Indians surrender their culture would not be satisfied with anything less than all-out retaliation.

Soon the cry went up, "Kill the whites and kill all these cuthairs who will not join us." When Little Crow did not agree immediately to lead the warriors, one man accused him of cowardice. Little Crow dashed the man's eagle-feather headdress to the ground. He spoke to the council:

Braves, you are like little children; you know not what you are doing. . . . The white men are like locusts when they fly so thick that
the whole sky is a snowstorm. You may kill one–two–ten; yes, as
many as the leaves in the forest yonder, and their brothers will not
miss them. . . . You cannot see the face of your chief; your eyes are
full of smoke. You cannot hear his voice; your ears are full of roar-
ing waters. Braves, you are little children—you are fools. You will
die like the rabbits when the hungry wolves hunt them in the
Hard Moon [January]. Taoyateduta is not a coward: he will die
with you.

Little Crow ordered that the attack on the Lower Agency begin
soon after dawn the next morning.

On the morning of August 18, 1862, the trader François La Bathe
stood in his doorway, smoking his pipe and admiring the rose-
tinted clouds just before sunrise. He had risen early, unable to
sleep because of the warm, humid temperature of the night before. He felt a nameless anxiety that morning, an unnatural stillness in the air that drew him to the door, to stand there watching
and waiting.

Across the river, just below the ferry crossing, Rosalie Marpiya
Mase knelt near LaCroix Creek, later known as Birch Coulee, to
fill her pail with water for cooking. Her youngest son, Oliver, a
sturdy baby nearly a year old, played with small rocks near the
edge of the stream. Although it was still cool in the shade beneath the cottonwood trees, the sun's heat had already dried the
dew on the long grass. Setting her pail to the side, Rosalie removed the carrying strap she wore for gathering wood and laid it
on the ground. Before she searched for the long sticks she used
for her fire, Rosalie knelt again on the uneven rocks that lined the
edge of the creek bed.

She bent low to scoop two handfuls of water to her face, closing her eyes as it ran cool and clean across her skin. A long braid
slipped over her shoulder as she looked carefully at her reflection.
She was a dark presence on the water, a shadow among the fragments of sunlight that caught the water streaming over rocks and

fallen branches. Her dark skin sometimes frightened the wives of the *wasichus*, the white men who traveled for days in wagons with their young brides and a few, meager possessions, to settle on the newly opened reservation land. One woman, whose skin and eyes were so pale she seemed ghostlike, had refused to leave her wagon and enter Rosalie's cabin, even though she had been invited to use their stove. Her husband tried to comfort her with clumsy words, "There's no call to be afraid. She ain't nothin' but a squaw, she can't hurt you none."

Rosalie stirred the water with her fingers, sending ripples through her reflection. There was no need to see how much her face had changed in fourteen years of marriage, especially after bearing seven babies. She sighed once, deeply, hearing the echo of her mother's voice in her breath: tired, resigned to what her life had become, yet caring for her family without complaint.

Settling her weight back on her heels, Rosalie rested, listening to the delicate sounds in the woods that surrounded this creek called by her husband's name, LaCroix. Her name now as well. She smiled, thinking it made no sense to name this water for a man. But white men did not understand the power that comes from naming something, from calling forth its essence and giving it a name, so that this child, or this river, or this moon can be known properly. When her babies were born, she had wanted to give them Dakota names. Without a proper name, the spirits would not recognize her children, they could not protect them from harm. Her husband had refused, saying his children would bear good Christian names and no other. She had no choice but to agree.

Turning to look at her youngest child, who now watched the hovering flight of a dragonfly near his head, reaching for the iridescent sparkle of its vibrating wings, she thought again of his name. Not his Christian name, Oliver, but the one she sometimes whispered to him as he slept. Her father, Iron Cloud, a war chief for Wacouta's band, had been renowned for his ability to dream, using these visions to find the enemy Ojibwe and foretell the outcome of battles. He had even claimed to know all about the fire canoe long before the first steamboat chugged up the river.

By the time Oliver was born in 1861, Iron Cloud had been dead nearly five years. When the woman who helped with the birth handed Oliver to Rosalie, she had looked down at his flushed face and watched how quietly he lay in her arms, as if already paying attention to the world around him. So unlike the lusty squawls of his older brothers, one of whom was already a soldier at the age of fourteen. Rosalie could not ask a medicine man to choose a name for her son, but she could whisper in Oliver's ear the name of his dead grandfather, so at least the spirits would know him. Perhaps he would even become a dreamer like his grandfather.

Rosalie spoke Oliver's name out loud, and he turned to his mother and smiled. His eyes shone with the same gentle warmth, although his skin was lighter and his body would one day stretch into the long bones of his French-Canadian father. Oliver reached one chubby hand for a rock that was almost too big for him to lift. His round cheeks flushed with effort while a strand of black hair fell across his eyes. Oliver was a quiet baby, learning his mother's silence on these trips to the woods. He watched her now as she sat with her eyes closed, becoming again all ears, a still, listening presence among the trees. Rosalie could hear the soft rub of leaves moving as birds searched for seeds in the brush, and the distant rustle of a deer that stepped lightly through the wild raspberries and tall sumac bushes.

A faint line formed along her brow, the fatigue evident from her sleepless night. It was hot and airless in the cabin, with the whine of mosquitoes a constant nuisance. The drums from Little Crow's village two miles further up the river had woken her, a familiar sound that usually she found comforting. But last night she was restless and uneasy. Early that morning she had discovered the dead body of a sparrow as she stirred the cold ashes of her fire, seeking enough embers to heat water for her husband's coffee. A dead bird in the house was a sign that death was near. She said nothing, but she watched her children carefully, praying for the son who had left the day before to fight against the Secessionists.

A shot rang out in the distance, startling Oliver and jolting

Rosalie into instant, focused attention. Had she imagined it? Was her older son already in the woods hunting for small game? No, there it was again. Another shot, and another. They came from the direction of the Lower Agency. Jumping to her feet and hastily placing Oliver on her hip, she ran clumsily down the edge of the creek toward the river, forgetting her pail and her carrying strap in her haste. Within a few minutes they were standing at the edge of the rapidly moving water, Rosalie breathing hard from her run and the fear that hurt her belly, Oliver clutching his mother's shirt in a small tight fist. They heard more guns fired, heard distant voices raised in terrible bloodlust as war cries were carried toward them on the west wind. Rosalie continued to stare across the river at the place not too far distant where she knew the Agency stood, as a thin line of smoke drifted upward from the area where the traders had built their stores.

Rosalie could see nothing and she heard no more guns fired. But she knew that this was the beginning of the end for all of them. This was the trouble she had seen coming once in a dream so terrifying she had spoken of it to no one, a dream where hatred covered the land like a flood and families were torn apart, where sons raised weapons against fathers, where brothers fought brothers to the death. The dream had begun just like this morning, with guns and smoke.

The underlying hate and resentment between whites and Indians was like dry tinder on the morning of August 18, 1862. It needed only the smallest of sparks to raise a flame from years of distrust, betrayal, and lies. Earlier that month, when she had visited her relatives across the river near the Lower Agency, she heard the men talking around the campfires. The young men argued that it was time to fight, while the old ones said they could not win a war against the whites. *Better to fight a losing war,* the young men shot back, *than to watch our children die of slow starvation at the hands of dishonest traders.*

Across the river Rosalie could see men moving in haste to push the ferry out into the water. She could hear their voices raised, shouting something in English, the language she still struggled to understand. She would not wait to find out what had happened at the Agency. She turned and ran as if her life was in danger, thinking only of her children.

Back up the hill at her cabin, Rosalie quickly handed Oliver to Lillia, her oldest daughter, and went in search of her husband. Louis was leading a horse from the barn, preparing to hitch it to the empty wagon that stood near the house. Rosalie ran up to him, her skirts trailing in the dust, and asked quickly, "What have you heard?" Louis said nothing for a moment as he concentrated on feeding the bit into the reluctant horse's mouth. Turning to Rosalie, he said, "Nothing yet. But I heard the shots, too many of them, over at the Agency." Louis's close friend and longtime trading partner, Louis Robert, had a store near the Lower Agency, along with Andrew Myrick and François La Bathe.

A few days earlier Rosalie had listened as Robert told her husband of the meeting he had had with the other traders, Little Crow, and the Indian agent, Thomas Galbraith. Rosalie stirred a pot of wild turnip and venison stew while the men spoke in low voices at the table. Robert said, "There's no telling when that money will show up. There's a war going on that is bleedin' the governments' coffers dry. Paying Indian money doesn't seem all that important to the folks in Washington just now. I told Galbraith, 'Our hands are tied. I can't afford to lend much more credit until that money comes in.'" Robert leaned back in his chair as a bowl of stew was placed in front of him. "Mark my words," he had said, raising his spoon. "There could be trouble."

As Louis continued to prepare his horse and wagon for travel, neither he nor Rosalie spoke of what might be happening at the Agency, but they both remembered Robert's words. They knew he was safe, for he had left the day before with the Renville Rangers, a group of fifty young men, mostly mixed bloods, who had been recruited to fight in the War Between the States. Their eldest son, Fred, at fourteen years old, had signed up to become a soldier.

"I'm taking no chances," Louis told Rosalie. "Pack only what you can carry, and quickly. We leave for the fort as soon as possible."

Rosalie turned without speaking and hurried into the house, calling her children's names quietly so she would not frighten them. Moving swiftly through the cabin's main room, she spread the nearest blanket on the table and quickly filled it with corn, beans, and a side of dry venison. As she worked she heard the sound of a man's voice raised in the yard.

Through the window she could see the ferry man, Oliver Martell, leaning from his horse, who still danced in the yard as if ridden hard from the landing. "The Indians have gone crazy killing all the whites and traders at the Agency," Martell said, his voice rising on a note of near hysteria. "The Reverend Hinman seen it with his own eyes, Indians hollering and shooting, bodies everywhere. Clear out as quick as you can," he yelled, turning his horse toward the road. "I'm off to Fort Ridgely to warn Captain Marsh."

Without seeming to hurry, Louis looked back once over his shoulder toward the house. Through the window, Rosalie saw his half turn and understood that it was time to leave. Turning to Louis, Jr., she said, "Take the little ones to the wagon." Louis grabbed his two younger siblings, Spencer and Adrienne, one in each arm, and carried them out. He quickly dropped them in the back and ran to the cabin once more for his prized possession, the rifle his father had given him on his twelfth birthday for shooting small game. Lillia and Ellen followed closely behind, Oliver still riding contentedly on his sister's narrow hip. Rosalie quickly folded her blanket around the food she had packed and climbed into the wagon. Louis flicked the reins across the back of their horse, and they rolled forward with a gentle lurch. Rosalie looked back once over her shoulder at the cabin she had lived in for more than fourteen years.

During that time, a small community of mixed-blood families, mostly French-Canadian fur traders and their Dakota wives, had sprung up around the LaCroixs. These families raised babies whose lives would forever be a contest, pulled between white and Indian culture.

She turned back to face the road that led toward Fort Ridgely.

Just as she had little choice about where they lived, it was not her decision whether they took refuge at the fort. Despite his years of living among the Dakota and raising mixed-blood children, Louis LaCroix sought his own community in moments of crisis. His survival depended on men like himself, who believed that the future lay in the hands of the white settlers and their government. He would defend his life and that of his family, to the death, if need be. Rosalie's moment of choice had come years earlier, when she married a white man.

As each passing mile carried them closer to Fort Ridgely, twelve miles east of their home, Rosalie moved farther and farther away from the reservation. The Dakota people had been pressured for decades to adopt white values, yet the Dakota War of 1862 was to place that decision in sharp relief, forcing individuals to choose sides. The struggle that many Dakotas felt at having to balance two cultures simultaneously came down to the gut-level decision of a single moment: *On which side do I make my stand?*

Living close to the ferry meant that the LaCroix family was one of the first to hear about the trouble at the Agency. Oliver Martell had already hurried off to raise the alarm at homesteads along the road to the fort. Rosalie could see strung out behind their own wagon two more filled with families. Another man led his horse while his wife rode, holding her baby. All of the men carried rifles or something heavy enough to be used as a weapon. Their wagon jolted over each rut on a dirt road baked hard by the sun, the horses pushed beyond their usual pace in such heat. Lillia and Ellen leaned against a hay bale, while the baby slept in Rosalie's lap. At the back of the wagon Spencer and Adrienne stared wide-eyed at their older brother, who whispered how he planned to single-handedly protect the family. All of them stared back at the home they had just fled, waiting to see if smoke would begin to rise from their own roof. Across the river it was clear that many fires were now burning, encouraged by the hot wind that had come up with the mid-morning heat.

More than once Rosalie searched the tree line for signs that the fires and the battle were spreading. As they rolled steadily toward the fort, she knew that on the opposite side of the river stood the villages of Traveling Hail, Wacouta, and Wabasha. She wondered how her own father, Iron Cloud, would have reacted had he lived to see this day. As a war chief, he was often antagonistic toward whites. Had he survived the cholera that killed him in 1856, would he now be among those on the other side of the river, shooting settlers and threatening to kill all the mixed bloods?

The last time Rosalie had visited Wacouta's village, an older boy who often called her "Auntie" had proudly displayed the duck he had shot himself, offering her part of his kill for her family. Whenever she could find time to visit, she felt immediate relief at speaking her own language, at sitting among women whose skin was as dark as her own. Rosalie thought of her relatives who still lived in the village, of her brothers and sisters who were now raising their own families, of her aunts and uncles and cousins, of the women who had come to deliver her babies. Where were they now? Were they preparing the camp for battle, rolling the bullets for the warriors' rifles, filling the air with their own ululations of war? Were they feeling the grim satisfaction that comes from finally confronting an enemy after years of lies and betrayals, countless humiliations, and the poverty of spirit and body that comes from depending on government handouts in order to live? Would she, Rosalie wondered, not feel the same way if she were still living in her father's village, rather than riding in the back of this wagon, surrounded by six of her children, whose blood was half Indian, half white?

By the time the LaCroix wagon reached the fort in late morning, the place was already swarming with young soldiers hurrying to prepare for their first real taste of battle. The Agency's boardinghouse operator, J. C. Dickinson, had escaped with his family and arrived first with news of the massacre. The fort's commander, Captain John S. Marsh, was an inexperienced young soldier in command of only seventy-six men. The day before, Lieutenant Sheehan had left the fort with fifty men of Company C, Fifth Minnesota, bound for Fort Ripley on the Mississippi River to serve in the states' war.

Louis escorted his family to the stone barracks reserved for women and children, returning quickly outside with his oldest son to offer their help in protecting the fort. Oliver Martell, the ferry man, whistled to Louis and said, "LaCroix, let's saddle up and see what we can find out." Louis told his son to help the men who were piling up dirt, stones, logs, bags of feed, and hunks of sod as makeshift barricades against the anticipated Indian attack.

It was already rumored that Little Crow would attack the fort with hundreds of his warriors. The fort was poorly constructed for actual defense, for it lacked a stockade and was surrounded by scattered buildings that were difficult to defend. On one side stood the barracks that housed the women and children, with the warehouse next door. Beyond that were the officers' quarters and a row of log houses used as a hospital and lodging for civilians. Several other buildings were spread out across the grounds, including the bakery, laundry, and stables. Even the site was poor, allowing plenty of cover for the Dakota to approach unseen in the ravines that surrounded it on three sides.

Looking around the dim interior of the barracks, Rosalie searched for familiar faces. Where was Nancy McClure Faribault, the mixed-blood Dakota woman married to the trader David Faribault? They lived just a mile or two down the road. Or Joseph Coursolle, a mixed blood married to a white woman, whose young daughters, Elizabeth and Minnie, often played with Spencer and Adrienne? All around her were white women with their children, women who kept a careful distance from her as they busied themselves rolling bandages. Rosalie was acutely aware that she had not pinned up her long braids, and they hung below her waist.

Rosalie found a quiet corner near the wall where she settled her children on the floor. Ellen whispered to her mother that she was thirsty. Spencer was standing nearby, restlessly shifting his weight from one foot to the other, resentful at having to sit with the women. Finding his mother's eyes upon him, he immediately took off in search of water outside in the courtyard, where the men shouted orders to each other. Lillia had already moved to sit with one of the older girls, while Ellen and Adrienne were irresistibly drawn toward the window, where they watched the men prepare for battle.

Several hours later Rosalie heard her husband's voice outside the barracks. Louis gestured to her from the doorway and they stood together for a few minutes. Louis's face was lined with fatigue and dust, his shoulders sagging as the horror of what he had seen began to settle into his body. He was over fifty years old, his muscles still firm from a lifetime of physical labor, but his strength was severely tested by these violent events.

"We rode nine or ten miles toward the agency," Louis said. "We didn't see nothing and it was all pretty quiet. About ten miles out we found three bodies on the road: Ed Mager, Smith, and another man. Looked like they just been killed. Me and Martell decided to turn back." Looking past her into the dim room, he asked, "The children?" She nodded her head. They were playing with friends in a corner while Lillia watched the baby. Louis touched Rosalie's arm briefly and then hurried toward the men, who were receiving orders for their positions defending the fort.

Toward evening a woman with disheveled hair and torn skirt was led in, the shock of losing her husband evident in the pasty white of her skin. She stopped at the doorway of the barracks, her eyes finding Rosalie in the dim light. For a moment she stared, then lunged toward Rosalie, her fingers reaching toward her face, her grief turned violent as she relived the image of her husband's death. She fell to the floor, restrained by two women who would not meet Rosalie's eyes.

One of the women left and returned several minutes later with the Reverend Samuel Hinman, the young Episcopal missionary whose efforts to learn the Dakota language had earned him many friends in the Indian community. Kneeling first by the woman whose grief kept her prostrate in wild, racking sobs, he quietly murmured words of comfort, all the while keeping hold of her hands. When once she half rose, pointing her finger toward Rosalie, he merely took hold again of her hand while gently shaking his head. Finally, she grew calm enough to sleep.

Rising wearily, for his day had begun with the massacre at the Agency, where he had barely escaped when the looting began, he made his way to Rosalie's corner. The LaCroix family were known as staunch Catholics, but they had met Hinman often at the Agency, where he lived not far from his church with his family. Years later one of the survivors would say of him, "If only the white people who treated the Indians so outrageously could have had the same ideals, the same love for God and their fellow men in their hearts, that terrible, never to be forgotten massacre would not have happened."

Sitting down next to Rosalie on the floor, his back against the cool stone like hers, he offered his hand, saying, "*Haw koda,* Rosalie." She bent her head in his direction, acknowledging the greeting. "I have seen your husband and son Louis out near the barricade," Hinman whispered. "Is your son Fred here as well?"

"He fights with the Renville Rangers," Rosalie said, her voice loud enough to be heard across the room. Hinman smiled and closed his eyes for a moment, sighing deeply.

"I fear for our brave Captain Marsh," he went on. "He did not seem to grasp the serious threat that waits for him and his men." Marsh had left around noon with forty-six of the soldiers, intending to reach the Lower Agency and put an end to the trouble. Before they left, Hinman had tried to warn Marsh that he would be outnumbered. The sun was now beginning to set and still no word had been received from them.

"I have seen terrible acts committed by men today," he said softly to Rosalie, as if talking to himself. "At the Agency they swore they would kill all the whites and the mixed bloods. If they had not stopped to plunder the stores, we would all be dead. I saw Myrick lying in his own blood, his mouth stuffed with grass." His voice trembled and he stopped speaking. "God help us all," he said as he stood up.

Before he turned toward the door a woman quietly touched his elbow. "Mary," he cried softly, gathering the woman's hands in his own. "Rosalie, do you remember my wife?" Mary bent and extended a hand to Rosalie. "Forgive me, Rosalie," Mary said, squeezing her hand gently. "But my husband is needed in the infirmary. One of the wounded is not expected to survive the night."

Throughout the evening refugees continued to arrive, many of them seriously wounded, carrying stories of near escapes. At last, after dark, the first two survivors of Captain Marsh's party arrived with the news of Marsh's death, along with that of twenty-three of his men, ambushed when they reached the Redwood Ferry. That terrible loss left the boyish Lieutenant Thomas P. Gere in charge of only twenty-two soldiers. Gere quickly dispatched a message to the commander at Fort Snelling asking for help immediately, instructing his messenger to also stop at St. Peter and urge the Renville Rangers to return to the fort. By this time, about 250 refugees had arrived seeking protection. The women and children were crowded into a single barracks, while a handful of men, some of them civilians, were posted outside, armed with hastily distributed muskets.

As the night wore on there was little sound inside the women's barracks except for the occasional hush whispered to a child who wept from hunger and fear, or a cry from one of the wounded. Rosalie could feel wakeful tension in the bodies scattered across the floor, some propped against the stone wall, others lying close to their children. All of them waited for the attack they knew must come, for the fort was the key to the Minnesota valley below it. Each one of them listened for the first war cry, the first bullet, the first sound that the battle had begun. Outside the barracks their husbands and sons stood fearfully, staring into the dark, straining tired eyes toward shadows that seemed to move. Each time one of the horses whinnied nervously from the stable, several rifles were cocked and ready to fire.

Just before dawn, Rosalie fell into a light sleep, her head slumped forward while her hands slowly relaxed on the blanket she had pulled around her shoulders. She dreamt she was home again in her mother's tipi, sitting in front of the fire while her mother combed her hair, braiding it with a long strip of red cloth, the color of women and the life force they carry in their bodies. *You are to be married,* her mother said, *to a Frenchman who will bring much trade to our tribe. You honor the family with this marriage,* her mother told her. Her mother finished braiding and sat waiting, silently, her hands folded in her lap. Rosalie knew it was time to leave.

She pushed aside the tipi door and stepped outside. Her father waited with the Frenchman, his gun set politely to one side. Rosalie turned toward her father, surprised to see his face painted for battle, his war club in his hand. With a terrible cry he raised his club and turned toward the Frenchman, who drew a long hunting knife from his belt and plunged it into Iron Cloud's belly. As he began to fall toward Rosalie, his eyes staring straight into hers, he slowly raised his arms like the wide wings of a crow preparing to fly away. His body rose up, caught by a current of air, and with a great cry he flew straight toward the sky. Above the trees a thin plume of smoke rose behind him.

Rosalie woke with a start, her heart pounding wildly in her chest. She understood what it meant to be here in this fort surrounded by white people and her own mixed-blood children. Somewhere in the fields and meadows that surrounded this area, her relatives would be among those who would come in the next few hours with guns and bows, determined to kill everyone who sought refuge in the fort. Her husband and her son waited for them with rifles cocked against the first shadow to move, their bullets not caring whether the flesh they tore might belong to one of her uncles, or even to the young boy who had shared his duck with her family. Surely her husband's Catholic God was right about the devil, and even to now he was riding throughout the land on his black horse, whipping men into a frenzy of murderous hate and revenge. She felt the chill of the morning settle into her bones, realizing that from this day forward her sons would find their lives forever changed in the moment they raised their guns toward the Dakota as an enemy.

Rosalie felt an almost hysterical desire to laugh, realizing the world had become so complicated that every enemy wore two sides to his face, one white and one red. The enemy was her family and no matter which way she turned, the enemy turned one side of its face toward her. She had honored her family by agreeing to marry the Frenchman but where was the honor in this early morning, when her husband and son lay waiting with their rifles? She knew there was nothing she could do now, nothing except hope that her choice would protect the young children who slept next to her and the baby who slept in her arms. But in the cold still moment before the sun finally broke above the horizon, casting its warm glow across a peaceful valley still shrouded in thin mist, she knew that she would bear no more babies for her husband. Let her son Oliver be the last of their family. She would bring no more children into a world where sons must fight against their own relatives.

3 *The Renville Rangers*

AUGUST 19, 1862
Fort Ridgely, Minnesota

About two days' march from Fort Ridgely, a group of fifty young men slept in an empty field outside of St. Peter, their thin blankets already damp with the dew that collected on the long grass. Exhausted from the day's march, they slept easily on the uneven ground. They were the raw, untrained recruits from the Upper and Lower Agencies who had volunteered to join the Union Army, calling themselves the Renville Rangers. Led by the Lower Agency Indian agent, Thomas Galbraith, and Lieutenant Norman Culver of the Fifth Minnesota, they had marched out of the Lower Agency at dawn on August 17, 1862, without rifles or uniforms, each man carrying his rolled-up blanket and holding his head high.

Rosalie's son, Fred LaCroix, was among these men. He was the eldest of seven children, accustomed to responsibility at a young age, and lacked the wild impetuosity that would later kill less cautious soldiers. Young, headstrong men like Fred and Augustin Frenier (Mazakoyaginape, Appears Clothed in Iron) from the Upper Agency were determined to test their courage in battle. They left their families to find glory as soldiers fighting in the war, having heard enough of the old men's stories of past victories. They were ready to prove themselves as warriors by defending their families and their land from the Southern rebels. Let their fathers and uncles decide who would turn their hands to the plow and who would hunt for game and move about the land as free men. The tribe had begun to divide amongst itself, forming a warriors' lodge that threatened harm to those who followed the teachings of the white man too closely. It was far better to look for battles outside the reservation.

Whatever fears each young man might have felt at night when he lay on his blanket with feet aching from a day's march of twenty to thirty miles, he kept them to himself. But when their sleep was broken before dawn by the sound of hooves clattering to a halt, when an overtired soldier nearly fell from his saddle, his muscles weak from exhaustion after hours of riding without rest, when he demanded to speak to Lieutenant Culver on a matter of great urgency, it was their first taste of the adrenalin that rises when battle draws near. Fred heard them speak in undertones made harsh with emotion. He watched their silhouettes gesturing against the faint light of a sky thick with stars as the messenger stood on legs trembling with fatigue, his body weaving slightly as he saluted. Culver asked what business brought him here in such haste.

"I regret to report, sir, that the Indians have broken out at the Lower Agency. They been killing settlers and looting stores. Captain Marsh and his men were killed, most of them anyway, ambushed by the Indians."

He patted his leather pouch, his fingers rattling the letter folded inside.

"This here letter warns the Governor about the trouble. I'm to ask you to return right now to Fort Ridgely. If you could spare a horse, I'll be on my way to Fort Snelling."

He drew in a deep, ragged breath and said, "May God be with you, Lieutenant Culver. The things I seen up there . . ." and he wiped the back of his hand across his eyes before turning to leave.

Fred saw the stillness in Culver's body as he absorbed the messenger's news, the last tendrils of sleep banished from his tired mind by the shock of the report. Culver turned to the soldier standing near his elbow and ordered him to rouse the men and prepare them to return immediately to Fort Ridgely. Most of the men had already heard the messenger's words. They rose quickly, rolling their blankets with hands made clumsy by the news, their eyes not seeing the task before them. Like Fred, these young men who had only just left home were now being asked to return and defend it. Not from the faceless enemy from the South, but from an enemy who was as familiar as the men who were their neighbors. Fred thought of his family living so close to the Lower Agency and wondered, briefly, before burying the thought, whether they had escaped. What would he return to?

Fred looked up briefly and met the same blank, worried expression on the face of Augustin, whose father, Xavier, lived further from the fighting but there was no way to know how far this would spread. What about his uncle, Narcisse, and his aunt Rosalie? Or her son, Denis Felix, his twenty-year-old cousin, who had already enlisted in Company A of the Sixth Regiment? Would they find themselves fighting side by side in an entirely different war?

They marched fifty miles that day, barely stopping to rest. Each young man was silent in his own thoughts, his worries about the family left behind made unspeakable by the fear that they might arrive too late. Armed now with muskets borrowed from St. Peter's storage, paid for with a $1,000 bond posted by Louis Robert, they marched with grim determination. Yet there was also a strong reluctance to face what they might encounter in the villages left behind. Most of these men were mixed bloods, their loyalties torn between family and tribe, between grandparents who admonished them to remember the old ways and ministers who exhorted them to protect their souls. By choosing to become Renville Rangers, they had thought to leave childhood behind, earning their reputations as men and soldiers fighting a common enemy. They had signed up to fight the white man in the white man's war, but they would be asked instead to raise their arms against their own family, no matter on which side they chose to fight, in a war that would sunder their community. It was the ultimate contest between the past and all of the history and traditions that belonged to the tribe, and the future, as defined by the whites' progress across the land, claiming everything in the name of civilization.

* * *

The Renville Rangers arrived at Fort Ridgely toward evening on August 19. They found the soldiers and families who had sought refuge there exhausted by a night of cruel anxiety, waiting for the attack they knew must come. Fred and the rest of the Rangers were immediately sworn in as privates in the army. With no time to rest, they were ordered into positions to help defend the fort. Fred could only look quickly around the compound for his family, just as every soldier swiftly scanned the corners for his mother, his father, and the young siblings he left behind. Some were greeted with a wave or a quick sign of the cross offered in silent thanks for the safe return of their son. Other families were absent: some killed, others taken prisoner and held at Little Crow's camp. Still others had picked up weapons and were among the warriors already gathering in the fields, preparing for the first attack on the fort. Later that night, several of the Rangers would silently leave the fort to search for their families or to join the warriors preparing to attack.

Near the stone barracks that housed the women and children, Fred saw his father leaning against the wall, his face lined with exhaustion. When their eyes met, Louis nodded his head toward the building behind him and smiled. Fred could feel his shoulders relax, relieved of the great worry he had carried since hearing the news of the fighting. His relief was short lived, however, when he caught sight of his friend Augustin, looking grim and alone. Fred's family might be safe, for the moment, but there were too many others around him still living in fear and grief.

When the first attack finally came on the afternoon of August 20, Fred fired without hesitation. Fear and adrenalin rose in his throat at the sight of Little Crow's warriors rushing toward the fort's outbuildings, firing guns and raising their voices in a terrible war cry. Whatever ambivalence he might have felt at firing toward men he knew, men he had grown up with, men who traded at Louis Robert's store or hunted with his father, he knew, with dreadful certainty, that they would kill him in an instant, kill his mother, his father, and his siblings. With a soldier's instinct to defend himself and his family, he fired and refired. When the shooting ended and the smoke from the cannon and the rifles began to clear, when the relieved silence of those who survived was broken only by the low moans of the wounded, then Fred bowed his head, no longer the naïve youth who had left home to become a soldier. He was a man, tested in battle, willing to kill to protect his family.

Later that night, Fred woke suddenly from the exhausted sleep his body had fallen into as soon as he lay down. His ears were still ringing from the gunfire and his shoulder ached from the kick of his gun. Turning his head, he saw the empty blanket next to him where Augustin had slept. Was he standing outside? As the minutes slowly passed, Fred realized that Augustin had deserted the fort. He must have waited until the guard was changing and there was a brief distraction as one weary soldier replaced another. If caught, he would be court-martialed. Fred thought of the warrior who had shouted earlier to the mixed-blood soldiers in the fort, "We will fix you, you devils; you will eat your children before winter." Rumors had already circulated that Little Crow intended to kill all of the mixed bloods. Augustin must be heading north toward the Upper Agency in search of his family.

From the bitterness that surrounded this brief war, a new priority emerged: protect the family at all cost. For a community that relied on the strength of its *tiyospaye*, or extended family, whose lives were governed by kinship rules that stressed the common good of the people, the Dakota War of 1862 was also a blow against tradition, against the peaceful heritage of kinship that had bound Dakota families together for generations. Assimilation had violated these kinship rules by forcing families to choose sides, placing the survival of individual families above the needs of the community.

By the end of the first week of fighting, the St. Paul *Daily Press* had embraced this bloody event with all the sensationalism it seemed to warrant. When the first story appeared within a day or two after the fighting began, it was brief, almost not believing that the situation could be as terrible as the early reports suggested. The fighting was described as an "outbreak," as if it had appeared out of nowhere, a sudden storm that had blown in from a cloudless sky. The newspaper promised more details as soon as it could gather information and verify it, relying on letters delivered by messengers who arrived breathless and weary from the long ride.

As soon as Governor Alexander Ramsey received his letter from Lieutenant Gere, he appointed Henry Sibley, a well-known fur trader who spoke the Dakota language, to head an expedition to stop this outbreak. Sibley arrived at Fort Ridgely on August 28 with 1,400 soldiers, six days after Little Crow's second, unsuccessful attack on the fort.

With each passing day, the stories spread across more and more of the front page, alluding to details too gruesome for the newspaper's readers' sensibilities. Headlines were stacked in bold type, one upon the next, declaring the latest bulletins from the front. "Battles at the Fort!" "Red Devils Repulsed!" Panic had spread rapidly throughout the area, extending far beyond the actual reach of the fighting. Letters were printed daily reporting fresh details from the war. Charles Roos, the sheriff of Brown County, wrote a letter to Governor Alexander Ramsey that declared, "The people here intend to kill every blanket wearing and arms bearing Indian who steps into Brown County."

Within days after the fighting began, columns were already devoted to scapegoating and finger pointing about who to blame. Nowhere was it suggested that this "outbreak" was the backlash of decades of mistreatment that included continual resettlement onto smaller reservations, broken treaties, starvation, and the ongoing humiliation of being treated as "savages." A great deal of attention was paid to whether or not the cash payment and annuity goods had been late—they arrived a day after the fighting began—suggesting that the delay might have been the cause for such an unexpected catastrophe. This simple analysis was soon overwhelmed by outrage fueled by the newspaper's report that hundreds of settlers had been killed, their houses and farms burned. The underlying motives were left for historians to judge.

* * *

Fred stood at his post near one of the outbuildings at Fort Ridgely, his new gun propped against his shoulder. His muscles ached from a long day of drills. Across the field from where he stood near the guardhouse, he could see the charred ruins of the stable and the sutler's store, which had burned in the second attack. Blackened wood posts stood in grim contrast to the fiery red of the sumac bushes that surrounded the fields. The cool nights of early fall had just begun to tip the leaves of the nearby trees a deep gold, a backdrop of startling beauty to the shallow, mounded graves that dotted the new cemetery.

In the month that had passed since Little Crow had attacked the fort with 800 warriors, Colonel Sibley had been determined to whip his green troops into a fighting army. Fred had learned to march, to crawl on his belly, and to fire his rifle from one knee. He had learned the golden rule of the military: thou shalt obey orders absolutely. He knew how to advance, to retreat, and to salute his superior officers. He had become a soldier in a very short time. Despite his newly acquired skills, the older soldiers who had come with Sibley still teased him about his few whiskers.

Stifling a yawn, Fred heard the lookout calling down to one of the soldiers in the parade area. "Two Indians coming on foot about a mile out on the creek bank." Colonel Sibley came to the door of his tent, rolling down his sleeves. He called out to the officer of the day, Colonel McPhail, to prepare a detachment of men to meet them.

His fatigue now completely forgotten, Fred joined the rest of the soldiers as they waited with sharp interest, some of them reaching for their guns, making sure they would be ready if they were needed. Colonel McPhail returned with the two men and escorted them directly into Colonel Sibley's tent. Fred knew one of the men as Thomas Robertson, a twenty-two-year-old mixed blood who spoke both Dakota and English, even accompanying his father as an interpreter to the treaty negotiations in Washington, D.C., in 1858.

After the tent door closed behind them, Fred called quietly to one of the soldiers who had been part of McPhail's detachment. "Pardon, sir," he said. "What's Robertson doing here?"

The soldier turned and looked at Fred, recognizing him as the gawky young man who worked hard during the day's drills, his fierce intensity making up for his lack of experience. It was obvious to him that Fred was young and a mixed blood to boot, no telling where his loyalties really lay, but since he had already fought in both battles at Fort Ridgely, he clearly had the makings of a soldier. Taking a few steps closer to Fred, he said quietly, "The half-breeds are here with a message from Little Crow. They were tight-lipped about what it said. Maybe the bastard's ready to give up." He spat at the ground in disgust and walked away.

Fred had heard the rumors that Little Crow's camp was filled with nearly 300 white and mixed-blood prisoners. Augustin's aunt, Susan Frenier, the Sisseton wife of former Indian agent Joseph R. Brown, was among them. Fred wondered if his friend had found his family; he feared that when this war was finally over, Augustin would be in a lot of trouble.

After several hours of questions about the safety of the prisoners, Thomas Robertson and the other messenger were escorted back outside the fort. They had delivered Little Crow's message refusing to surrender the prisoners. Robertson had also handed over a letter written in secret from Chief Taopi, who wished to be taken under Sibley's protection. Sibley sent a stern message back to Little Crow warning him that he must give up the prisoners. To Taopi, Sibley replied that he would soon be on the march and they should gather the prisoners into a separate camp. "All those that have committed murders and other outrages against the Whites will be punished. All those that have been friendly and acted as such will be duly considered and protected."

Within days of Robertson's visit, Fred received orders that the soldiers would leave Fort Ridgely to pursue Little Crow and negotiate the safe release of the prisoners. Early on the morning of September 19, an army of 1,600 soldiers, including Fred, one of thirty-eight Renville Rangers, headed upriver. After four days of easy marching, they made camp in a rough triangle near Lone Tree

Lake. Confident in the superior strength of their numbers, they set up cooking fires and unrolled sleeping blankets, neglecting to post guards at a distance from camp. During the night, over 700 Dakota warriors crept to within a few miles of their encampment. Little Crow's plan was to ambush the soldiers in the morning when they were strung out along the road.

Unaware of the danger that surrounded them, Fred searched the rows of soldiers for Denis Felix, a cousin of Augustin, hoping to hear what had happened to his friend. Just as dusk was beginning to blur the features of the men around him, he saw Denis sitting on the ground with some of the other soldiers from the Sixth Regiment. Catching his eye, Fred lifted his chin in a nod of recognition. Denis left his group and came forward, offering his hand in greeting. Neither asked the obvious questions, waiting instead for information to be offered.

"My family made it to Fort Ridgely," Fred said. "When I last saw them they were safe and well. Worried, of course, about their neighbors and relatives." Fred thought briefly of his mother's dark skin amid a barracks crowded with white settlers, another worry that he was reluctant to face.

"My mother is safe with our family in Mendota," Denis said, referring to Rosalie Frenier Felix. "My uncle Narcisse may be at the Upper Agency. I've had no word about him or his great-uncle, Louison. He is an elder and cannot move as quickly as he used to." Many of the Frenier family lived near the Upper Agency.

Fred nodded his head, relieved that Denis's family had thus far survived. As the silence stretched between them, he could not resist asking in a low whisper, "And Augustin? Is there any word?"

Looking briefly around them before he replied, Denis said, "Only that he has deserted his post. I hope for his sake that he is far from here."

In the morning, a few hungry soldiers decided to gather potatoes from the nearby gardens without first asking permission. Driving their wagons straight across the fields, they nearly ran over the Dakota who were lying hidden in the grass. The warriors were forced to leap up and fire, losing the element of surprise. After two hours of fighting, the Dakota withdrew, a decisive loss that marked a turning point in the war.

Following the battle, the split between the hostile Dakota and those who wished to make peace widened even further. While Little Crow and his warriors were fighting, the Dakota who opposed the war took control of the captives and brought them into their own camp. When Little Crow returned defeated from Lone Tree Lake, those who opposed him sent word to Colonel Sibley that he could come for the prisoners. Little Crow fled north with about 150 followers, while other Dakota escaped to Montana or crossed the Canadian border.

On September 26, Fred LaCroix and Denis Felix were among Sibley's soldiers who set up an encampment just north of the camp where the prisoners, both white and mixed blood, were held. When Sibley marched in with his army, he immediately released the prisoners.

The 1,200 Dakota who were also present surrendered to Sibley, trusting his word that they would be treated fairly. They were told that their annuities would be paid but that first they would have to be counted. The men were asked to give up their weapons with the promise they would receive them back. As soon as they were disarmed, they were immediately placed in custody at a separate camp nearby. Over the next few days more Dakota continued to give themselves up, swelling their numbers to about 2,000. Despite assurances of fair treatment, all the Dakota, regardless of their involvement in the fighting, many of whom had helped white settlers survive, were held prisoners under armed guard. Meanwhile, as soldiers continued to search the area, a mass trial began almost immediately of the warriors who had taken part in the war.

In his new role as a private in the army, Fred was kept busy on guard duty around Sibley's encampment. Any feelings he may have had at seeing so many Dakota held prisoner nearby despite Sibley's promises of fairness, he kept to himself. Fred stayed at his post, holding his rifle with a tight, anxious grip, and did as he was ordered. Only when he saw Susan Frenier Brown among the released captives did he reveal the trace of a relieved smile. At least Augustin's aunt was safe.

He saw Denis Felix only once in the days that followed, when he was coming off duty and headed toward his tent. Just beyond a group of soldiers playing cards around a low-burning fire, Fred saw the familiar loping gait of Augustin's cousin. Ducking around the hindquarters of a dozen horses, he quickened his pace to catch up with Denis before he vanished in a milling crowd of soldiers and former prisoners still waiting to go home. As he drew abreast of Denis, Fred reached out to touch his shoulder to catch his attention. Denis turned quickly, a fierce glare on his face, ready to confront whoever had intruded on his private thoughts. At the sight of his face, Fred dropped his hand and took a step back. Seeing that it was Fred who had stopped him, Denis immediately reached out to shake his hand.

"*Haw koda*, Fred," Denis said, gripping his hand tightly. "Forgive me, I didn't see you standing there. I have a great deal on my mind."

Fred began to ask what was worrying him so, but a look from Denis stopped the words before they reached his lips.

Denis asked, "Are you headed toward your tent? I'll walk with you."

They fell into step, a silence lingering between them. As the number of men around them began to thin, Denis spoke quietly, without turning his head. "Have you heard?"

Fred shook his head, not understanding the question.

"Well, you will soon. There are trials already being held at La Bathe's home at the Lower Agency. You knew this? They try men like cattle, one after another. Any Dakota who held a gun is sentenced to hang." He drew in a deep breath. "They caught Augustin. He is among those sentenced to hang. As a deserter."

Neither man spoke for a long moment. Denis said, "I hear talk that the prisoners will be moved to Mankato. They're not safe here." Fred and Denis knew they guarded the prisoners more for their own protection from angry whites than to prevent them from escaping. After all, where would they go? What would they eat? Many of them had surrendered because they were starving.

"And the others?" Fred asked, thinking of the nearly 1,700 women, children, and elders who waited in a camp nearby. "What will become of them?"

"They will move to Fort Snelling before winter," Denis replied. "The government thinks they'll be easier to feed there." *And to protect as well* was his unspoken thought. Being female brought no measure of safety to an Indian. Shaking his head, Denis turned without another word and abruptly walked away.

Fred stood without moving and stared after him. Was it true? Augustin, a Renville Ranger like himself, would now hang? Despite his training as a soldier for whom desertion was considered the ultimate act of cowardice and betrayal, he knew that Augustin had left Fort Ridgely to find his family. He could not stay and fight when his family was in danger. And for that he would hang.

As the bustle of the military camp continued to flow around him, Fred struggled to make peace with his decision to fight alongside white soldiers. Too many lives had been lost on both sides for him to see a clear right or wrong in this war. He had lived all his life among white men, and he saw how they dominated everything, from the business of trading to government to the military. He would be part of that, as he had been raised.

On the morning of November 7, with a cold wind plucking at his wool coat, Fred watched while a long, slow line of Dakota people began to leave the nearby camp. He saw old men shuffling in worn moccasins or riding in the few wagons that carried their meager belongings. Children clung to their mothers' hands, their heads uncovered, their cheeks already stung red by the wind. Most of all, he saw women marching with grim determination, some with babies on their backs or held on one hip. With their men imprisoned or hunted like animals on the prairie, these women carried the uncertain future of the Dakota nation in their arms.

When the wagons reached Henderson, one of the marchers said, years later, "We found the streets crowded with an angry and excited populace, cursing, shouting and crying. Men, women and children armed with guns, knives, clubs, and stones rushed upon the Indians, as the train was passing by, and before the soldiers could interfere and stop them, succeeded in pulling many of the old men and women and even children from the wagons by the hair of the head, and beating them, and otherwise inflicting injury upon the helpless and miserable creatures.

"I saw an enraged white woman rush up to one of the wagons and snatch a nursing babe from its mother's breast and dash it violently upon the ground. The soldiers instantly seized her and led or rather dragged the woman away, and restored the papoose to its mother—limp and almost dead. Although the child was not killed outright, it died a few hours after. The body was quietly laid away in the crotch of a tree a few miles below Henderson and not far from Faxon.

"I witnessed the ceremony, which was, perhaps, the last of the kind within the limits of Minnesota; that is, the last Sioux Indian 'buried' according to one of the oldest and most cherished customs of the tribe."

When the prisoners finally reached Fort Snelling a week later, they were confined in an overcrowded camp of tipis on the north bank of the Minnesota River, surrounded by a wood fence to protect them from marauding parties of white people. Many of the Dakota who had surrendered because of starvation were exhausted to the point of collapse by the long march from the Lower Agency. They were told to surrender their medicine bundles and sacred objects, all of which were burned in a large fire. Missionaries, including Samuel Hinman, immediately began the work of converting the vulnerable prisoners to Christianity. About 130 Dakota would die that winter from exposure to cold and the spread of measles and other diseases. Those who survived waited anxiously to learn what their fate, and that of their men, would be.

On November 9, the condemned men were moved to Camp Lincoln at South Bend. As they passed through New Ulm, Sibley and his troops had to mount a bayonet charge to drive back the whites who were determined to attack the prisoners with rocks, bricks, and fists. Fearing violence from a mob of white citizens, Sibley later transferred the prisoners to a more secure prison at Mankato.

President Lincoln approved death sentences for thirty-nine of the 303 Dakota who had been condemned, one of whom was reprieved at the last minute. During the week preceding the executions, missionaries succeeded in baptizing most of the men. On December 26, 1862, thirty-eight prisoners were marched from the prison and hung, surrounded by 1,400 soldiers and a hostile crowd of white civilians. The men who were reprieved from hanging, including Augustin Frenier, were sent to a prison in Fort Davenport, Iowa, in the spring of 1863.

The hanging did little to satisfy the lust for revenge that still consumed settlers. They demanded that any Indians who had escaped be pursued and punished and that the 1,700 Indians held at Fort Snelling be forcibly removed from the state. On September 9, Governor Alexander Ramsey had announced, "The Sioux Indians of Minnesota must be exterminated or driven forever beyond the borders of the state." Ramsey eventually declared a

Fort Snelling prison camp, winter 1862–63

$200 bounty for the scalps of Dakota people who had eluded capture. During the following year Colonel Sibley continued to pursue the Dakota who had escaped. Little Crow was shot and killed near Henderson in July 1863, while picking berries with his son, Wowinapa.

In his official report on the "Sioux Uprising," agent Thomas Galbraith offered this recommendation for the Dakota: "The power of the government must be brought to bear on them; *they must be whipped, coerced into obedience.* After this is accomplished, few will be left to put upon a reservation; many will be killed; more must perish from famine and exposure, and the more desperate will flee and seek refuge on the plains or in the mountains. . . . A very small reservation should suffice for them."

Political parties echoed these sentiments, passing federal legislation in February 1863 that broke all treaties with the four bands of Dakota Indians, including all rights to land in Minnesota, and approved the use of the remaining funds to reimburse the losses of white settlers. In March 1863, additional legislation arranged for the removal of the Sisseton, Wahpeton, Mdewakanton, and Wahpekute bands and the sale of their lands.

Acting hastily and with limited funds, a new reservation was chosen near Fort Randall in the Dakota Territory, at Crow Creek. In the spring of 1863, the Dakota who had survived the winter at Fort Snelling were loaded onto overcrowded steamboats and transported down the Mississippi River to St. Louis, then up the Missouri River to their new home.

When the Renville Rangers disbanded in the fall of 1862, Fred enlisted with the First Minnesota Mounted Rangers, a twelve-company regiment recruited to capture Dakota people who had fled to Lake Traverse, north to Canada, and west into Dakota Territory. Fred fought in the battles of Big Mound, in North Dakota, and at Stony Lake. At the war's end, when the long pursuit of escaped Dakota was declared over, Fred rejoined his family at their original home site in Morton, Minnesota.

An uneasy peace settled on the state in the aftermath of the war. White settlers moved back to the land they had abandoned and made claims on the repossessed reservation lands. As they continued to move farther west, other Dakota tribes rose up in a few desperate attempts to staunch the overwhelming flood of white settlers on Indian land.

Years later, fingers would be pointed between the Mdewakanton and the Sissetons about who was really to blame for starting the war. The word "traitor" was used to describe those who had refused to fight against the whites, the "friendlies" who had helped protect the white prisoners, and the scouts who had assisted the soldiers in tracking down hostile Dakota when they fled after the battle at Lone Tree Lake. Some would be so hated that they could no longer live among their own people. The deep, anguished schism created by the war was another blow to the Dakota, whose culture was structured around kinship and acting as good relatives. The issues that ignited the violence and the grief that burdened all those who participated, regardless of side, soon became secondary to the immediate struggle for simple survival.

4 *Sisseton to Santee*

APRIL 1884
Santee Reservation, Nebraska

On an early spring day in mid-May, 1863, a season of hope and re-
newal when even the dry plains bloom with new life, the steamboat *Florence* made its slow ascent up the Missouri River. Among
those on board was the missionary John P. Williamson, who had
continued his religious work among the Dakota throughout their
imprisonment in Minnesota. In a letter to his mother, he com-
pared this final leg of the journey to Crow Creek, when all 1,300
prisoners were crowded onto one boat, as "nearly as bad as the
Middle Passage for slaves." After the long winter months at Fort
Snelling, the prisoners were emaciated and ill, and soon after
their arrival, the hills surrounding the reservation had become
covered with graves. Williamson would later say, "The very memory of Crow Creek became horrible to the Santees, who still hush
their voices at the mention of the name."

The next three years may well have been among the darkest
period in the history of the Dakota as they struggled to survive on
the edge of starvation and disease. They had been banished to an
inhospitable area described by the Indian agent as a "drought-
stricken desolation, a land with no lakes, almost no timber—the
whole country being one wilderness of dry prairie for hundreds of
miles around." The land was already suffering from a deep cycle of
drought, so no crops could be harvested in the first two years. Yet
they were forbidden at first to leave the reservation to hunt. They
relied on emaciated cattle provided by the government, along
with rancid pork and flour, and women were forced to turn to

prostitution to keep themselves and their children alive. Many people died from disease and malnutrition; by 1865 only 1,043 Indians remained at Crow Creek, more than 900 of them women. After three years, it was said that 600 children had died.

Finally, in the spring of 1866, after an official report deplored the state of semi-starvation at Crow Creek, a new reservation site was chosen in Nebraska, just below the South Dakota border. With few supplies on hand, the elders were sent forward by wagon, while the rest of the semi-starved Dakota walked one hundred miles to Niobrara, where they were reunited with the men who had been imprisoned at Davenport. There the Dakota families lived in tents while the missionaries and other whites stayed in a hotel nearby.

While an improvement over Crow Creek, much of the new Santee reservation was suitable only for grazing. Nonetheless, this was the new home for the Santee Sioux, or Dakota—the place where they would begin to rebuild their devastated lives and community.

Rosalie Marpiya Mase and her mixed-blood children were not sent to Crow Creek. While her eldest son pursued escaped Dakota across the plains, Rosalie remained in Minnesota, along with a handful of other Dakota who were allowed to stay. Many of the scouts and their families settled near Big Stone Lake, near the border between South Dakota and Minnesota, where Louis died in 1874.

The Sissetons and Wahpetons, many of whom had nothing to do with the war, settled on the Couteau des Prairies, not far from Big Stone Lake, after the government tried and failed to have them removed to Crow Creek with the Mdewakanton and Wahpekute. In 1867, a treaty established the Sisseton reservation, and Gabriel Renville was elected its chief. Under Renville's leadership, the Sisseton reservation became fairly successful at farming while maintaining the Dakota language and traditional customs.

In the spring of 1884, Rosalie's youngest son, Oliver, lived with his brother Fred and Fred's wife, Millie, in their small house on the Sisseton reservation. Oliver remembered nothing of the war except moving frequently in the years that followed. After his father died, Oliver moved to Sisseton with his family, where he learned to play the fiddle and enough basic carpentry skills to earn a living.

Early one morning, Oliver stood in the open grass near his brother's barn, tightening the straps on his saddle. In one of his saddlebags he had a parcel of food from Millie. As Oliver turned to pick up his fiddle case, he saw Fred standing near him, his large hands holding the case with delicate care. Oliver had tried to convince both Fred and Louis, Jr., that they should come with him to the Santee reservation in Nebraska. Their sister Lillia was already living at Santee with her husband, Charles Mitchell, and their children. It was rumored that land would soon be allotted in 160-acre parcels, two years ahead of allotments on the Sisseton reservation.

Both brothers had turned him down. They were married, with families of young children, and they preferred to wait until Sisseton allotted its own land. As a former soldier, Fred felt more comfortable among the Sisseton, who were not as traumatized by the war and its aftermath. He knew that some still blamed him for his part in the fighting. He believed that the war had hurt everyone, whites and Indians, and the quicker it was over, the better it was for everyone. Here, at Sisseton, he lived near other former soldiers and scouts, like the Renvilles and the Robertsons. He had married Amelia Mitchell—Millie—and started a new life. He had even given the census taker his Dakota name, *Cuske Tanke*, or Eldest Son, a tradition that his family had given up long ago.

Oliver swung one long leg up and over his saddle. Fred looked up at him, shading his eyes from sun, and said, "I'd be glad to hear word of Augustin, if there is any news to tell." Oliver nodded his head and turned toward the south. He thought briefly about his mother, who worked at one of the reservation schools, and wondered if he would ever see her again. With a nudge in his horse's side, he followed the wagon tracks that led him away from Sisseton and his family.

* * *

"I beg your pardon, ma'am, I mean, Miss," Oliver said, nearly blushing beneath his dark skin as he stammered a greeting to the woman standing in front of him.

Jenny Felix smiled in return. She was intrigued by the young stranger who was so clearly flustered in her presence. He was new to the Santee reservation, although she had already heard stories that a handsome LaCroix had recently arrived from Sisseton, riding a horse with a fiddle case strapped on its back. Here he was, striding out of the agency building, nearly running her down in his hurry.

Hastily pulling his hat off his head and stuffing it in his pocket, Oliver said, "My name is Oliver LaCroix. I'm new around here."

"Come for your share of the land?" Jenny asked. Her parents, Peter (or Pierre) Felix and Margaret Bellecourt Felix, had moved to Santee from Mendota in 1883 for the same reason. Minnesota was still considered a hostile place for Indians, although more and more Dakota were returning home. The Felix family also wanted to see their relatives, who had been living at Santee since they were removed from Minnesota in 1863.

"If it's true," Oliver replied, relaxing a little. There was something very appealing about this eighteen-year-old woman who stood so confidently in front of him, a smile lighting up her eyes, as if she was about to laugh at some shared joke between them. So many people at Santee still bore the scars of the 1862 war and the horrific years that had followed at the Crow Creek reservation. It seemed that everyone had lost family. Oliver could look in a person's eyes and see the inconsolable pain of having watched a child starve to death.

In 1873, a smallpox epidemic had devastated the Santee reservation, and many people left their homes, some never to return. The reduced size of the Santee community was heralded as a victory for white settlers, who seized more and more of the surrounding land. Following the massacre of Custer and his soldiers at Little Big Horn in 1876, there was another failed attempt to have the Dakota removed to another reservation. With all the un-

Jenny Felix, probably 1880s

certainty surrounding their future, complicated by frequent crop failures caused by drought and grasshoppers, the Dakota made only slow progress toward the economic self-sufficiency the government hoped for.

In the years that had passed since the Dakota arrived empty-handed at Santee, fields had been plowed, and the Santee Normal Training School and many homes were built. Samuel Hinman, who had followed the Dakota from Fort Snelling to Crow Creek, had moved with them to the Santee reservation. With his usual tireless zeal, he soon built a school and church, only to see them, and many of the reservation's newly erected buildings, destroyed by a tornado in 1870.

By 1884, when Oliver arrived, the displaced Dakota had begun the difficult work of creating a new community. The task of erecting buildings and schools was far less daunting than the effort needed to recover from the trauma of the war, the forced march that sent them in exile from their homes, the loss of ancestral lands where their relatives were buried, and the years of starvation and loss at Crow Creek. Some couldn't face what they had been through and chose to hide in bootlegged whiskey smuggled onto the reservation. Their faces had the haunted look of men whose dreams wouldn't let them rest.

"The agency is giving me work," Oliver said. "Next week I'll start building some of them new houses. If I get a piece of land, I'll build my own place someday." For a moment that thought hung between them, electric with possibilities. Jenny abruptly turned, saying over her shoulder, "Good luck, then," and began to walk briskly away.

"Wait a moment, miss," Oliver called. "What's your name?"

Jenny hesitated and turned back around.

"Jenny Felix."

"Are you kin to Denis Felix?" Oliver asked.

"He's my uncle," Jenny replied. "He lives down the road with his family, not far from here."

"I'm supposed to ask if anyone around here might know something about Augustin Frenier."

"Well, I'll have to think a minute," Jenny said. Tapping her finger on her cheek, she considered Oliver in silence. "I believe Augustin came here not long after the war. I don't know what became of him after that." Augustin was among the men whose death sentences had been remanded to a prison term at Fort Davenport instead. It was rumored that his uncle, Antoine, the interpreter, had been killed by his own people for telling lies during the trials.

Jenny smiled once more and walked away. After a few steps she stopped and asked, "Do you like to fish?" Without waiting for his answer, Jenny turned back down the path. Oliver watched her go, admiring the straight line of her small back, her tiny waist, and the self-conscious tilt of her head. As if feeling his gaze, she glanced once over her shoulder before hurrying down the path into the woods. The deep green of the cottonwood trees seemed to swallow her up as she disappeared from sight. A warm breeze fanned Oliver's face, reminding him that the day was growing late and that he still had much work to do.

By 1890, Oliver LaCroix and his bride of three years, Jenny Felix, were living on their 160-acre allotment near Howe Creek. Jenny's parents, Peter and Margaret Felix, lived nearby, as did a number of Freniers and Felixes. Oliver's land was marginal for farming, but it was good enough on which to build a farmhouse for the large family they planned to raise. They had a two-year-old son, Oliver, Jr., and Jenny was already pregnant with their second child when Oliver staggered through the door one night in December. His eyes were wide and unfocused, and his hands trembled as they reached for the cup of hot coffee that Jenny placed on the table. Sitting across from him, Jenny waited patiently until Oliver was ready to talk.

"I heard . . ." he said, and then he could not speak for the emotion that choked his voice. "I heard today, at the Agency, that there has been a great slaughter of Lakota people on the Pine Ridge reservation." And then he spoke no more and buried his face in his hands.

Slowly, over the next several days and weeks, Oliver and Jenny heard the full story of what had happened at Wounded Knee, a camp about two hundred miles west of the Santee reservation.

In the years since the 1862 war, the Lakota tribes had continued to battle government soldiers while the flood of white settlers encroached on their land. Finally, they had turned to the Ghost Dance as their last hope of salvation. When their great leader, Sitting Bull, was killed, they fled by the hundreds to seek refuge at one of the Ghost Dance camps or with Red Cloud, a chief on the Pine Ridge reservation.

An ailing chief, Big Foot, fled with a hundred or so of his people toward Red Cloud's camp at Pine Ridge, shortly after Sitting Bull was shot and killed. Big Foot and his people were overtaken by soldiers who were under orders to arrest Big Foot. As dusk fell across the low South Dakota hills, Big Foot was ordered to make camp on Wounded Knee Creek. When the prisoners were settled, they were counted: 120 men and 230 women and children. Two troops of sentinels were stationed around the tipis, and two large guns were positioned on the rise overlooking the camp. In the morning the male prisoners were told to gather in the center of the camp and surrender their arms. A young warrior, Black Coyote, refused to give up his rifle. As soldiers struggled to take it away from him, the gun went off. The soldiers responded immediately. The Indians, who were now unarmed, began to run. The guns on the hill opened fire, raking the camp and killing men, women, and children. When the shooting ended, Big Foot was dead, along with 153 of his people. Many more crawled away to die later, raising the count to nearly 300 people killed. The wounded Lakota were loaded into open wagons and driven to Pine Ridge.

Years later, the Oglala medicine man Black Elk would say of this battle, "When I look back now from this high hill of my old age, I can still see the butchered women and children lying heaped and scattered all along the crooked gulch as plain as when I saw them with eyes still young. And I can see that something else died there in the bloody mud, and was buried in the blizzard. A people's dream died there. It was a beautiful dream. . . .

The nation's hoop is broken and scattered. There is no center any longer, and the sacred tree is dead."

The Wounded Knee massacre was a crushing blow to the Dakota nation. The cries of those who died that cold December day reverberated for thousands of miles. There would be no repercussions for the soldiers who had taken part in this massacre. This was the final battle in a war that had been fought since 1862. As snow covered the mass grave that had been dug for the hundreds who died, a wave of grief spread throughout the country. It continued to ripple outward for decades, waiting for a generation who would finally demand their own reconciliation.

The news spread across the Santee reservation, and those who still remembered the 1862 war closed their eyes in renewed despair. The young ones vowed revenge, but there was no spirit left for war. The elders said, "It's no use."

The white man had won.

As Oliver moved through each day with a feeling of heaviness in his chest, he thought of his brother Fred. He had come home from the war a changed man. Although Oliver had been just a child then, he remembered his brother's silent moods, the private pain etched across his face. He had seen too much of the butchery that men unleashed against each other in the name of war. At night, Oliver could hear Fred call out from the dreams that haunted his sleep. He wondered now if Fred still heard the cries of the wounded, the sharp crack of a rifle, the sickening sound of a bullet entering flesh, and remembered an enemy's face that looked so much like his own.

Oliver had heard from other soldiers that men in the military regarded Indians as less than human. He suspected that his brother, and many of the Renville Rangers, had come home from the wrong war. Rather than fighting in the Civil War, Fred had fought against the Dakota at a time when the Dakota nation was torn between its traditional culture and the overwhelming pressure to adapt to the white man's ways. The 1862 war had been as much a struggle for the soul of their nation as it had been a war against the whites. With the massacre at Wounded Knee, decades of bloody struggle between whites and Indians for power, for control of land, and for one culture's right to dominate another, were over. For many of the Dakota, their own personal war was just beginning.

As the long years of fighting finally ended, the fear and distrust between whites and Indians deepened into unforgiving condemnation on both sides. The weapons of war were replaced with an insidious racism that had been present since the government's earliest dealings with Indians, a weapon that proved to be the most destructive of all.

In the fall of 1907, when a thin blanket of snow covered the hills after a stretch of cold, freezing weather, Oliver LaCroix stood about to cross the Niobrara River with his horse and sleigh. A pile of lumber was stacked behind him for his next project as a carpenter for the Agency, work that supplemented the meat and vegetables that he and Jenny raised on their farm. They kept a few cows, pigs, and chickens, with a large vegetable garden on the sunny side of the house. Their large family meant that Oliver and Jenny worked all the time just to feed their children. Jenny made bread nearly every day, and they drank all the milk that their cows could provide. Oliver and his older sons had already brought home several plump pheasant and grouse, while the girls dug wild turnips and potatoes from the garden. With luck, the winter would be mild, sparing them the unpleasant surprise of finding one of their cows frozen near the fence line.

With so much of the Santee reservation suitable only for grazing, and that only when there was sufficient rain, Oliver was fortunate that his carpentry skills allowed him to support his family. He continued to build frame houses throughout the reservation, replacing the tipis that many had lived in after moving from Crow Creek. In those years in winter, the women used to cut long slough grass and pile it around the base of their tents in an effort to make them warmer.

Oliver's horse picked a careful path through the reeds frozen at the edge of the river just as the sun broke through a thin layer of clouds, its bright light reflected off the dull blue of the ice. Oliver hummed a favorite fiddle tune, his voice a low rumble that set his horse's ears twitching. He thought about his older children who were away at school. Oliver, Jr., attended the Santee Normal Training School, while Henry was studying at Haskell. Henry was the smart one in the family, the boy who would do well in school. Oliver's twelve-year-old daughter, Maude, was sorely missed as a favorite companion by the younger children while she was at school. With her sweet disposition and quiet manner, she would do well in her nurse's training.

As Oliver approached the river crossing, he wondered briefly if the weather had been cold long enough to freeze a thick layer of ice. With his hands already nearly frozen inside his mittens, he decided that he would take his chances. Flicking the reins on the back of his horse, he set off across the river. Oliver couldn't help feeling pleased at his progress. At this rate, he would be home well before dark.

The sound of ice breaking reached his ears first, followed by the sharp cry of his horse as its legs hit icy water. Down it went, hind quarters disappearing into the dark as the sleigh followed. "Gee up," Oliver cried, hoping to spur his horse to a last valiant effort back onto the ice. Within seconds, the water closed around the sleigh and its heavy load of lumber. Immediately his skin felt the stinging of water too close to freezing for him to survive long. Already his pants, boots, and coat were beginning to drag him down. Clinging to the side of the icy hole, he heard a welcome shout in the distance. After what seemed like the rest of his life, a rope appeared near his stiff arms and a voice entreated him to hang on. Barely conscious, his lips already blue with cold, he wrapped his fingers around a knot in the rope. Slowly, painfully, he felt his body move inch by inch onto the frozen surface of the river.

"Good God, man, what were you thinking crossing the river this early in the season?" A voice resonant with irritation and relief cut through the fog that had begun to dull Oliver's thinking. "We've got to get you out of here before you freeze to death."

By the time Oliver reached home, he could no longer feel his feet or fingers. Each breath in his lungs was sharp and painful. Jenny swiftly stripped the now-frozen clothing from his body while she ordered her son to build up the fire. Wrapping Oliver's body in blankets as he began to shake uncontrollably, she brewed a pot of water for medicinal tea. When the shaking had subsided, Oliver was helped to bed, where he lay under a thick pile of blankets with a mustard plaster on his chest.

Despite Jenny's efforts, within days it was clear that Oliver was seriously ill. Although he was only forty-five, his body was worn from hard labor. Jenny sent word for her oldest children to return home from school immediately; she needed Maude's help with the younger children. Oliver grew steadily worse. He died shortly afterward.

As the word of Oliver's death spread through the Santee reservation, family and friends appeared with gifts of food and blankets, offering anything they could spare to help the family through this difficult time. Jenny was now a widow and the sole support of nine children.

* * *

Cupid Busy
LaCroix–Dion

On Tuesday June 15, 1915 at Niobrara, occurred the marriage of Miss Maude LaCroix of Niobrara to Mr. Paul Dion of Burke. Miss LaCroix was quite well known in this vicinity and is recognized as a fine young woman of worth and intelligence. Paul, we all know as a wide awake young man, always in good cheer and pleasant to meet. He is just out of school and now, with a good companion, enters upon life in real earnest and with promising prospects. The Gazette joins their many friends in wishing for this happy young couple, the best that life affords.

Paul Dion spent a few extra minutes one morning combing his hair and wiping the trail dust from his boots. He was on his way to work at his father's roller rink on the main, and only, street in downtown Burke, a small town about a hundred miles west of Santee across the South Dakota border. His parents, Oliver Dion and Susan Langdeau Dion, owned a large and sometimes prosperous cattle ranch on allotment land near Whetstone Creek, Miyogli Wakpala, three miles north of Burke. Paul's family was mixed blood, or *iyeska*, enrolled on the Rosebud reservation.

The roller rink was Oliver Dion's latest scheme for making money while the cattle industry continued to struggle. Ranching was backbreaking, dangerous work filled with disappointment from unpredictable cycles of drought, locusts, and dust storms. Paul was not a gifted horseman like his father or his oldest brother, John. He rode hard but he had also broken his share of bones rounding up the cattle that grazed their land. It was a pleasure, then, to spend a few hours working inside the roller rink. Especially since he had run into an attractive young woman who was visiting from the Santee reservation. Her name was

Oliver and Susan Langdeau Dion and family, after Mass, about 1905

Maude, and he had invited her and her friend to visit the roller rink today.

Now Paul stood behind the counter and handed pairs of roller skates to the few townspeople who were curious enough to try this game. With one eye on the wood floor where just about everyone landed on their first time around the circle, he kept his other eye on the door. Late in the afternoon, as Paul was beginning to lose hope, he straightened up from lacing skates on a young boy just in time to see the door open.

With the afternoon sunlight casting its bright aura around her head and shoulders, Maude LaCroix entered the rink. She stood for a moment in the doorway as her eyes adjusted to the dim light. With her high collar and cinched-in waist, Maude was feminine, self-possessed, and immensely attractive. She carried herself with a calm air, seeming reserved but not at all shy. Paul noticed, too, that she was quick to laugh. When she stood near the counter waiting for her skates, he was drawn to the gentleness in her eyes and the elegant line of high cheekbones in her strong face. At twenty-three, he had spent a rough life as a cowboy, and he yearned for something beyond long days in the saddle, listening to his father's whip-sharp voice calling orders to his sons.

Within the year, Paul and Maude were married on the Santee reservation. Maude's mother, Jenny, was living with her eldest son, Oliver, Jr., and his wife, Mary Hinman, on Jenny's land. No allotment land remained at Santee after it was opened to white settlers, so Paul and Maude moved back to Burke to await the birth of their first child, Margaret May Dion, in May 1916.

5 *Jousting with Windmills*

AUGUST 1991
Holy Rosary Mission School, South Dakota

Somewhere near the South Dakota border, my eleven-year-old daughter stated, "I am never going on another road trip with you, ever again."

We had been driving all day in midsummer heat, the wind blasting us continually through the open car windows. We were sweaty and covered with a fine layer of highway dust, exhausted from four nights of camping in a warm, humid tent, and more than a little tired of each other's company. She had expected a vacation filled with swimming pools, the Corn Palace, and a little souvenir shopping at Wall Drug. I thought I was giving her a sense of her own history, a glimpse of the landscape and small towns where her ancestors once lived. While she felt betrayed by her mother's boring ideas, I was drained by the effort of driving over 1,500 miles in five days on a journey to the past that I had not consciously intended to make.

Five days earlier, just after the sun rose on another humid August morning, we had loaded our tiny car with a tent, sleeping bags, and a black cast-iron skillet. I had told Jodi that we were going to camp in the Black Hills. She filled her backpack with clean clothes and a book, stuffed her purse with her carefully saved allowance money, and told her best friend that she was going on vacation. I had a road atlas and the dangerous idea that South Dakota held the key to my mother's history and her story about Holy Rosary. While I was raising my own daughter, I struggled to understand how my grandmother Maude, whom I knew to be a kind woman, could leave a child behind when she and her family moved away. Finally, at the age of thirty-six, I was heading to South Dakota, driven by a restless, wordless need to learn something, anything about the past.

Once we crossed into South Dakota, I left Interstate 90, the freeway that runs directly into the Black Hills. We headed south, traveling more slowly on two-lane roads with little traffic beyond the occasional farm tractor piled high with bales of hay. We drove for eight hours that first day, trading Minnesota's lush farmland for the plains of South Dakota, its rolling hills covered by a thick layer of goldenrod. We spent our first night in a deserted campground on the edge of Burke, a tiny town near the land where I had been told that my great-grandfather, Oliver Dion, once owned a cattle ranch. We had no time to look around, as there was barely enough light to pitch our tent on uneven ground. I could sense Jodi's concern about the way the vacation was going. I assured her that things would improve.

The next day we drove through much of southern South Dakota. We stopped briefly in St. Francis, a small town on the Rosebud reservation, where five of my aunts had lived at the St. Francis Mission School in the 1920s and 1930s. Margaret, Agnes, Midge, and Florence spent at least seven years each at St. Francis, all of them living at the school from the age of five. My aunt Pauline had lived at St. Francis during the fourth grade.

My daughter and I drove past the school, pausing only to admire the lifeless form of a rattlesnake sprawled across the entrance to the parking lot. I remembered my mother's warning not to camp in the Badlands because of the snakes. I thought how this scene typified South Dakota to me—a tranquil and beautiful land on the surface, but somehow neither safe nor welcoming.

Leaving St. Francis, we pushed further across an increasingly bleak landscape where little grew except long tufts of buffalo grass. The sun was high overhead when we stopped at Wounded Knee. As we walked toward the monument, where a handful of people were standing in silence, I told her about the massacre of nearly 300 Indian men, women, and children in 1890. She listened quietly, a look of anguish on her young face, before asking if she could buy a can of pop at the stand near the bottom of the hill. We drove in silence for the next few hours, both of us subdued by the unrelenting heat and the almost palpable sense of South Dakota's oppressive history.

We turned into the empty parking lot at the Holy Rosary Mission School late in the afternoon. The sun was still intensely warm, raising a shimmering wave of heat from the pavement. After we parked in the shade of the tall pine trees that stood in front of the main building, my daughter and I sat without speaking, hearing only the tick of the engine as it cooled and an occasional sigh of wind through the trees. I could see a sign near the front door that read, "Welcome, Red Cloud Indian School, *Mahpiya Luta Owayawa,*" renamed since the years when my mother lived here. This was the place I had been looking for, the unacknowledged destination on this whirlwind trip.

In front of us stood several austere, two-story brick buildings: the main office, the visitor's area, and a heritage center. To the left was the Catholic church, with double doors and a tall steeple, the white cross at its peak standing in sharp contrast to the vivid blue sky behind it. A sign pointed up the hill toward Red Cloud's cemetery. We saw no other visitors, or staff, or students; the benches along the sidewalk were unused, the doors and windows on every building were closed. The school stood empty and isolated, set back from Highway 18 by a long driveway, four miles from Pine Ridge and 700 miles from our home in St. Paul, Minnesota.

"Jodi," I said in a loud voice. "This is where your Grandma Cille went to school."

"What," she replied, pulling the Sony Walkman from her ears. "What about my grandma?"

"When grandma was your age, around eleven, she stayed here the whole school year. She didn't get to go home and see her family."

"Grandma Cille?" With a child's innocent self-absorption,

she sounded surprised to hear that the woman who breaded pork chops to such startling perfection might have had an earlier life.

Jodi started to raise her earplugs, but I spoke quickly, hoping to hold her attention with an impromptu lecture on what little I knew of our family history. "One afternoon, Grandma and I were sitting at the kitchen table talking. I used to ask her questions about boarding school but she didn't like to talk about it. She used to say, 'We were poor.'"

"Grandma was poor?" It was hard to imagine my mother not living in her comfortable home with my dad, their freezer packed full and a year's worth of canned goods in the cupboard. I was a single mother, so Jodi knew about frugality, why there were no motel rooms for us on this trip. But neither of us knew about living poor.

"So I kept asking questions, pestering her," I explained. "She said that the older girls used to go to boarding school because their family couldn't afford to feed them."

We sat in silence for a long moment. I knew that Jodi hated to see anyone suffer, especially her grandmother, who had helped take care of her when she was a baby. Jodi was her first grandchild and those early years of undivided attention had created a close bond between them.

A thin thread of sweat began to trace the outline of my stomach. I kept looking at the steps of the church, steps that my mother had climbed every morning on her way to Mass. I had been imagining this place ever since I had first heard of it as a teenager, had felt its strong pulse in my mother's past, in her reluctance or inability to talk about her early life.

I turned to look at my daughter. Her cheeks were flushed and her bangs stuck to her forehead. I reached out and tucked a long strand of hair behind one ear. We had several hours of driving ahead of us before we could set up our tent in the Black Hills.

I had no idea what to do now that we were finally here. We just sat in the car, limp, looking at the buildings, the pine trees, and the statue of an Indian saint by the side of the driveway. There would be no tour, no questions asked and answered, no details to replace the scenes in my imagination. What had I hoped for in coming here? The questions that had gone unasked twenty years earlier now swarmed like black flies in June, biting, pinching, difficult to ignore and even harder to escape. I knew that my mother did not have the words to tell me what I needed to know. Coming to Holy Rosary was a simple, unconscious declaration that I needed more than I had been given.

"Mom," Jodi said, a desperate tone creeping into her voice. "Can we go swimming now?"

6 The Sixth Daughter

South of the Missouri River along the route once followed by Lewis and Clark, the tiny farming community of St. Helena, Nebraska, had been built on a hill with a commanding view of the river valley below. Cedar and juniper trees softened the surrounding hills, where deep shadows carved a female contour in the landscape.

In the mid-1800s, St. Helena was a "port of entry" for the hundreds of emigrants who came directly from Europe via the Missouri River. Many of them continued to head west across the formidable expanse of Nebraska's tallgrass prairie and through its often inhospitable weather. Soon after Nebraska Territory was organized in 1854, settlers discovered that its soil was rich and fertile. The first group of settlers came from Minnesota and claimed land, building sod houses, raising families, and planting acre upon acre of corn and wheat.

Life was rigorous—the hard work of breaking sod for farming, enduring the cycles of drought and locusts—but it also promised a future for those strong enough to endure. Soon white farmers dominated the landscape around St. Helena, while Indians lived on marginal land in the nearby Santee and Winnebago reservations.

By the summer of 1925, farm commodity prices had fallen drastically, while costs had shot up, causing a nationwide farm depression. Paul Dion sold part of his 156 acres of land near his father's ranch in Burke and leased out the rest, relying on the

65

payments to help support his family while he searched for whatever work he could find. Three daughters were born at Burke: Margaret, Agnes, and Florence; Midge arrived in Bloomfield, Nebraska, in 1920; and their fifth daughter, Pauline, was born in Rosebud in 1923. Soon Paul was moving his large family from farm to farm as they followed the rhythm of the seasons: branding cattle, sowing crops, and reaping the harvest.

When Paul heard that a white farmer near St. Helena had work, he hurried to the man's farm before someone else could be hired first. As they talked, the farmer pointed at the small cabin down the road to which Paul could bring his family. The farmer looked Paul over and was reassured by his hard-calloused hands, the knotted muscles in his forearms where his sleeves had been pushed up, and the quiet look in his blue eyes. Paul was light-skinned, his features revealing more of his French ancestry than his Indian blood. Paul answered questions with a slow nod of his head, one hand rubbing the back of his neck while the other rested in the pocket of his well-worn overalls. He needed this job to feed his family, especially with another baby on the way.

Later that afternoon, Paul rolled up to the cabin with his wife and a wagon full of brown-eyed girls, their skin darkened by the sun, their eyes half-hidden by hair that gleamed black from a distance. The farmer shook his head and muttered to himself, *I've hired a half-breed and his squaw.* Living this close to the reservation, he sometimes had to rely on Indians to get his crops in during the fall harvest. Most of the time they worked hard. Still, it wouldn't hurt to have a word.

He chose a moment when they were riding back from a tour of the fields to say, "I've got no place for shiftless drunks here." Paul didn't answer. He simply looked out across the freshly turned furrows still dark with rain. He knew what the farmer meant.

At the end of the harvest, when long rows of corn filled tall silos and hay was rolled in neat bundles to dry in the fields, the farmer allowed Paul and Maude to stay in their small cabin through the winter and wait for their baby to arrive. The cabin was forty miles from the Santee reservation where Maude had been born and where her father Oliver had died. Last she heard, her mother, Jenny, and two of her younger siblings had moved to Lead, South Dakota, looking for work in the gold mines. Everyone was struggling to survive. Her family relied on the garden produce that Maude canned and the root vegetables she stored in the coolest corner of the cabin. She and Paul planned to stay through the spring planting and then move again, looking for work along with many other families.

At least this corner of northeast Nebraska offered fertile fields where a decent crop might grow with a bit of luck and some reasonably good weather. This area had not suffered the devastating droughts and grasshopper infestations that had driven them from their land in South Dakota, where many farms had simply gone into foreclosure, taking with them a high number of failed banks.

The struggle to support their family had forced Paul and Maude to enroll their two oldest daughters, Margaret and Agnes, at the St. Francis boarding school on the Rosebud reservation. St. Francis had been built at the request of Chief Spotted Tail in the late 1800s, when he realized that it was impossible to win a war against the whites, that his people would need to learn the whites' language and their ways in order to survive. Paul and his brothers had also attended St. Francis, which was free to children with at least one-quarter Indian blood.

The previous September, Paul had borrowed a hay wagon and driven nine-year-old Margaret and her seven-year-old sister, Agnes, up to school. The girls didn't want to leave home, knowing they wouldn't return until the following June. Two days before they left, while Maude was still mending socks and searching for a pair of shoes that would fit Margaret's growing feet, Agnes had stopped eating. She picked listlessly at the boiled potatoes on her plate and complained that her stomach hurt.

Maude had quit stacking plates and sat down next to Agnes, studying her face. All of her daughters showed early promise of the beautiful women they would become, but even then, Agnes was exceptional. She struggled not to cry, her eyes shining with unshed tears. There would be no one to say goodnight, no younger sisters to tease, and a locked door at every turn. Maude listened and said nothing, familiar with the ache of homesickness that Agnes was already feeling. She knew, and Agnes knew, that in hard times, you did what you had to and you made the best of it.

Early in the morning on March 27, 1926, long before the sun rose on fields of frost-covered stubble, Maude counted the seconds in the interval between the pain that had awakened her and the one that followed. Soon her water would break, her body a practiced chute at delivering babies. Maude knew her husband loved his daughters but hoped his sixth child would be a son, someone who would work beside him in the fields and eventually help support the family.

In the cabin's main room, three daughters lay huddled together in a single bed placed close to the wood-burning stove for warmth. The fire had burned down to a few embers during the night. Maude could see her breath in that room, feel the late March freeze, reminding her that winter was not yet over despite the occasional thaw. Just two days earlier, Maude had hung the family's clothes out to dry when the sun had shone with a promise of spring warmth, raising buds on trees and drawing farmers to stand in their doorways, looking out at still-frozen fields.

With a sharp intake of breath, Maude felt another labor pain move through her body. Paul stirred, rolled to his side, and fell back into a deep sleep. Maude heard her two-year-old daughter, Pauline, whimper as the blanket she shared with her sisters was pulled away, exposing her round legs, covered only by a thin nightgown. If this coming season were as hard as the last one, then Pauline's two older sisters, Florence and Midge, would also leave for boarding school in the fall. Just over four years old, Florence was still little more than a baby herself, and Midge was only a year older. They helped take care of Pauline, amusing her with dolls made of corn husks and rags. Maude heard Midge asking Pauline what was wrong. The mattress rustled when Midge moved to cover her baby sister with the blanket, and then silence filled the cabin again.

"Paul," Maude whispered in a low voice, not wanting to wake the girls. "It's time." Paul grunted and rolled on his back briefly, rubbing his tired eyes.

"Run up to the house and get one of them to come help. Ask if they'll mind the girls 'til this is over."

Paul slid cold legs into his pants, found his socks, tucked in yesterday's shirt, fastened suspenders over his shoulders, and placed his beloved hat on his head. Pulling the collar of his coat high around his neck for warmth, he stepped out the front door. Paul breathed in a sharp bite of air and stood for a moment looking at a sky still thick with stars. Another baby on the way, another mouth to feed, another body to clothe, another worry if he allowed himself to feel it. Nothing to be done about it now. Except pray that the birth went well, sparing his wife any unnecessary pain. He started up the hill, feeling the nearly constant pain that had settled in his joints, even though he was still a young man at thirty-four. A lifetime of rounding up horses, branding cattle, working in the fields from sunrise to sunset had aged his body quickly. There were days, already, when rising from his bed required an act of sheer will.

The night ended quickly in a flurry of preparations for the birth. Two neighbor women arrived with their hair hastily pinned up, their faces worn with fatigue. One woman kept an eye on the girls, who were awake and calling for their mother. The other went immediately to Maude's side, ran a practiced eye down the length of her body, and rolled up her sleeves to work. Every few minutes a wave of pain would draw lines on Maude's silent face. The cabin was quiet except for the crackle of the fire now blazing in the stove and an occasional deep, labored breath from the bedroom. Before another hour had passed, before the sun had begun to brighten the low rolling hills of the Nebraska horizon, Lucille Irene Dion was born. Her hair was black, her face flushed with her first cry, surprised to find herself so suddenly in the world. After the baby was bathed and swaddled in a well-worn quilt, Lucille was laid on top of the warm, soft mound of Maude's stomach. Paul came in with the three youngest girls and they stood peering at their new sister. She was tiny and perfect, her eyes squeezed shut in a round, birth-mottled face, her miniature fingers rolled into a fist.

When Lucille woke to find all of these eyes holding her, she remained calm, like an old soul gazing from a new body, her shell-pink ear pressed against her mother's heartbeat. She lay quietly, listening to the rhythm that had formed all of the days and nights of her short life, connecting her to generations upon generations in a family whose past stretched far beyond memory.

On this cold sunrise in 1926, Paul and Maude faced a mounting anxiety over how to feed their growing family today, and tomorrow, and the day after, when there was very little work to be found. On his next trip to the Rosebud Agency to collect their lease money, Paul would enroll Lucille into the Rosebud tribe. She, too, was now eligible to attend reservation boarding schools.

7 A Steady Paycheck

OCTOBER 1931
Lead, South Dakota

Each morning shortly after daybreak Paul Dion picked up his metal lunch box and miner's hard hat with a small light fastened to the front and joined a stream of men walking slowly toward the locked gate that guarded the Homestake Mining Company in Lead, South Dakota. A steep road led through the gate and down to a valley where large flat buildings contained the real business of gold mining, where men laboriously dug hundreds of miles of underground tunnels with mechanical rock drills and shoveled ore into cars by hand.

A flatbed truck was waiting on the other side of the gate, its motor running, as the gate was unlocked. Men crowded onto the back of the truck, some sitting along its edge with their legs dangling over the side. The scratch of a match and the hurried intake of breath as a last cigarette was smoked broke the silence. English miners from Cornwall, who had earlier worked the Michigan iron mines, sat alongside Finns who had come to log timber for the mine shafts. The truck was filled with a mix of Italian, Chinese, German, Scandinavian, Indian, African, and Slovenian workers, their communication sometimes limited to hand gestures and a few basic words of English.

Paul sat quietly, his eyes following the horizon until it disappeared from view. By the end of each shift, his lungs wheezed and struggled for breath against the dust and humidity of the mine shaft.

Inside the building, Paul switched on his light and stepped

into the small elevator car that carried him to the tunnel, where he would spend the next eight hours. He had nearly forgotten his first day of work, when the prospect of spending all day in a tunnel raised such terror that he almost turned and fled. As a cowboy and ranch hand, he had been surrounded by an infinite horizon on South Dakota's flat plains. He could break wild horses, herd cattle, and toss a rope with enough accuracy to ride in a rodeo. He knew how to plow a field, spending long days squinting into sun that sometimes raised a mirage out on the hard-baked fields. And he knew about wind, how it could pick the topsoil right off your fields and leave it on another man's farm, and then turn around with a cloud of locusts ready to devour an entire crop of wheat.

None of that had prepared him for the dark, damp smallness of a tunnel.

He learned early to send his mind away, to close himself off from the dirt walls that surrounded him. He began to dream, to think of the business he would one day own, something that didn't involve backbreaking labor. There was a side to Paul that was sensitive and delicate, a side that Maude had understood when she agreed to marry him. *Something will turn up*, he thought, *if I can just get ahead a little bit.* In the meantime, he had a steady paycheck and that was all that mattered.

There was no room for regret in Paul's life, no part of him that liked to go back and wonder if he should have stayed on the land he once owned not far from his father's ranch. Since his daughter Lucille's birth five years earlier, they had moved from farm to farm across Nebraska and South Dakota. Their daughters' birthplaces marked the itinerary of their travels.

Just as the struggle to feed his large family began to seem nearly impossible, a letter came from Maude's mother, Jenny LaCroix, who was moving back to Mendota with her younger children. They had been living in Lead, South Dakota, where her son Clarence had found work with the Homestake Mining Company. Gold prices were rebounding and the company was hiring, raising Paul's hope of steady work.

The Dion family moved to Lead in time to welcome their seventh daughter, Norma Grace, who was born on August 22, 1930. Now they were settled in a house with a chicken coop—and the miracle of indoor plumbing!—and for once they didn't have to worry about how they would pay their bills.

Just beyond the Dions' porch railing, down three wood steps worn bare of paint, the road led to a tall hill that had been sliced in half, known as the Open Cut. The naked eye could see a rough road that wound halfway down the hill before it switched back and then curved away to a distant floor, where a truck seemed the size of a matchbox. The town of Lead—a word that refers to a ledge or outcrop of ore—was nestled in the northern tip of the Black Hills, also known as Mile High City for its altitude. Lead grew up around the mining company after the Manuel brothers found their "home-stake lode," in 1876, shortly after the Lakota were forced to sell the Black Hills. Everything in this town, including the houses built into the hill like tiered seats in a movie theater, grew out of the gold mining business.

Upstairs in the bedroom, Margaret woke slowly, still tired from a long night of dancing at the Fireman's Pavilion. Three of her younger sisters—Agnes, Midge, and Florence—were at school at St. Francis. They had made friends in earlier years, and they chose to return to St. Francis rather than attend public school in Lead. Margaret, the eldest at sixteen, had taken a year off from school to help her mother with the baby, Norma.

Finally she got up from her bed, found several sheets of paper on her desk, and began to write a letter to Agnes.

Dear Sister,

I thought I would give you a break and drop a few lines to let you know I'm still alive and still percolating.

How is everybody down there? I supposed everybody is OK like they are up here. Lucille sure is fat and Topsy [Norma] is getting as wide as she is tall. I'm getting skinnier than I was when you last saw me. Mother and Dad are fine.

I sure got a break the other nite down to the dance. They had judges during a certain dance pick out the prettiest girl on the floor and she was supposed to pick out the ticket for the car that was to be given away. Boy! Maybe you can imagine how surprised I was when after that dance they announced that "'Miss Margaret Dion is the prettiest girl on the dance floor and is given the honor of drawing the tickets for the New Ford V8."'

I got me a new dress and hat. They are brown and they match my brown shoes, sox and gloves. I'm going to send you my red and white outfit but listen if you let every girl in the school wear it you won't get any more clothes. And most of all don't give it away like you did with that other outfit and for goodness sake take care of it. We are going to send you your package as soon as possible that'll be some time this week.

How is sister Baptista getting along now. Who is your needle-work teacher this year?

Do you like school this year? I suppose you do. We got Cille's report card this morning and it was a good one. She had all B's.

Well sis I must close here with love.

> Your Loving Sis, Margaret Dion or Wampus, Pakahantus,
> Squaw, Brown Eyes, Bright Eyes, Poky, Smiles or Marge.

Her letter finished, Margaret wandered downstairs and took the baby, Norma, for a walk in the backyard while Maude washed clothes in her machine and hung them outside to dry. As Maude dropped clothes into the soapy water, she thought about the report card for Agnes that had come in the mail. The letter stated that although Agnes was considered a "bright scholar," her grades were disappointing. At fourteen, she was clearly rebelling in the only way she could. Girls were forbidden to date at school but Agnes was rumored to have a number of admirers, teenage boys who were drawn to her brilliant smile. With a sigh, Maude wrung water from Paul's shirt, seeing only her daughter's strong, stubborn chin and defiant expression.

A letter would have to be written, and soon. It was so hard with the girls away at school and no way to talk with them directly. Maude could only remind Agnes of the high marks she had the previous year and encourage her to improve. If she could find a bit of time, Maude would also send a package of home-made jams and a new blouse. Maybe she could ask Margaret to walk to the post office later and mail her letter.

Norma played quietly in the sparse grass, making handfuls of dirt and twigs that she tossed in the air. Margaret leaned her face back into the sun, nearly dozing for a few minutes. She woke to the hissing of raw dough as it was dropped into a pan of hot grease. Before long, the fragrance of freshly made fry bread wafted into the backyard, a sign that Pauline was expected home shortly from school, and Lucille from her quick trip to the store to sell a basket of eggs. Soon they would burst through the front door, Pauline chattering away as always. A plate of fry bread was waiting for them with a pitcher of maple syrup to drizzle on top and fresh milk from the neighbor's goat.

Deep in the earth, far below the house where his daughters ate their fry bread, Paul leaned his shovel against the tunnel wall and wiped the sweat from his face. His breathing was shallow, his shoulders raising with the effort of each breath. Closing his eyes against the pain, Paul willed himself to keep working. The relief of a paycheck was far greater than his fear of pain.

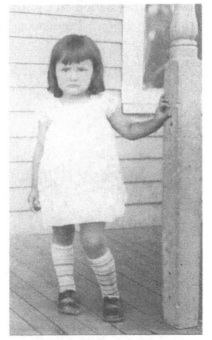

He continued to work until one afternoon when a section of the shaft crumbled, sending hundreds of pounds of rock hurtling toward the miners, breaking Paul's foot as he leaped for safety. He knew that he was lucky to be alive.

Later, when his foot was healed, Paul returned to work. *Lucille Dion, about 1931*

His asthma, which had improved while he was recuperating, grew rapidly worse. The company doctor warned him that he had to quit because of his health.

In early 1933, Maude wrote to Agnes at St. Francis,

> Agnes if I had money to send you girls I would but I haven't any. Times are not so good as they used to be. That's all we hear over the radio is that cattle & horses are dying all over the state they have nothing to feed them. So I guess we should be thankful we have food and shelter.

By this time, South Dakota had plummeted into a devastating depression. Farm foreclosure rates had risen even higher after the state was hit by a severe drought in 1933. Returning home to Burke was out of the question, as the droughts had transformed that area into a dust bowl. Feeling they had no choice, the Dion family sold their house and moved to Rapid City, where Maude's brother, Oliver, Jr., might help them find work. Before they left, however, they added an eighth daughter to the family: Darlene Rose was born on November 22, 1932.

8 Hard Times

AUGUST 1936
Rapid City, South Dakota

A relief administrator from the federal Works Progress Administration (WPA) stood alone in the middle of an empty South Dakota field early one August morning. Instead of the tall corn that should have been near harvest, the field had been mown to a stubble, with scraps of husks all that remained from the cloud of grasshoppers that had devoured the crop overnight. A warm chinook wind blew from the west, raising dust devils in the distance as it leached any remaining moisture from the soil. Although the hour was still early, just past 9:00 AM, a rim of sweat was already forming beneath his hatband. Shaking his head, he thought about the report he would have to file back at the office. "Crops are in the worst condition I have ever encountered." From Mobridge to Aberdeen, it was doubtful if a single field would be harvested that summer.

His office had already been swamped with reports of grasshopper damage and burned crops from farmers throughout the region. One farmer told him with a glint of grim humor in his eye, "The hoppers in this area are so numerous that they could do considerable damage to crops if there were any crops to damage." Nor did they limit their destruction to field crops, also mowing down garden vegetables, vines, and hedges. Scarcely a green leaf was left after the grasshoppers were finished.

Less than five inches of rain had fallen in the past four months, while temperatures climbed well over 100 degrees for a record number of days. The wind was so hot that any remaining crops simply withered in the field where they stood. Everywhere that his eye could see, there was only the devastation that follows drought and insects. The unrelenting sun had baked South Dakota's soil hard and dry as a bone. The entire state was dormant, ravaged, and desperate.

President Roosevelt had already ordered federal agencies to provide assistance to the state. The WPA stepped in with projects building farm-to-market roads and water-conserving dams and offering aid to at least 100,000 farm families. But even that would not be enough to prevent farmers from leaving for other states. There was little vegetation for cattle to graze on and no hope of a grain crop to sustain them over the winter. The government had already bought one million head of cattle and shipped them to other states for feeding. A headline in a Nebraska newspaper read, "Thousands of Catholics in Nebraska Knelt at Special Masses Yesterday to Pray for Rain."

Over half of all farmers were receiving emergency relief, with South Dakota claiming a higher percentage of people on relief rolls than any other state. But by far the worst conditions existed on the state's Indian reservations, where people suffered from startlingly high rates of poverty, disease, and death.

In a recent letter to her daughters, Maude had written,

> Margaret, I wrote for your rent money and it came yesterday, but Dad used it, the car was broke down and also my wash-machine and I still have to use the board to wash on and that is all cracked, but I guess I'll have to do the best we can. Daddy hasn't any work yet and we are still on relief.

After Paul and Maude moved to Rapid City, they both worked wherever and whenever they could. They found jobs with the WPA, and then Paul worked on a road crew, in a canning factory, as a volunteer fireman, and finally for a dry cleaner. Always good with his hands, Paul learned tailoring work quickly, finding satisfaction in the artistry involved in making straight seams and crisp corners, eventually learning to embroider exquisite linens as well. When the Dions couldn't find work, they lived on the small relief checks that the government provided.

Maude's older brother, Oliver LaCroix, Jr., also known as Uncle Smoky, lived nearby with his wife, Mary Hinman, and their nine children. Pauline and Lucille played with their cousins, Agnes and Art, in the woods that ran behind their house. The two families shared what little they had, including the commodities handed out by the government: canned meat and grapefruit and lard to make sandwiches with sugar.

By the summer of 1936, Margaret had moved out with her future husband, Agnes was living at home, and Midge and Florence had just graduated from St. Francis. Pauline and Lucille were on vacation from public school, helping care for the little ones: Norma, Darlene, and the family's last child and only boy, Paul, Jr., known as Sonny, who was born on July 1, 1934.

On the evening of August 19, after a sultry day when the air was still and heavy with humidity, Pauline and Lucille watched their older sister Agnes curl her hair with rags and carefully out-

Dion family in Rapid City, 1936: left to right, Pauline, Maude, Paul, Midge, Lucille, Florence, with Darlene and Sonny in the front

line her lips in a crimson that sparkled against her dark hair and eyes. Agnes chatted with Florence and Midge as she dressed, asking about teachers at St. Francis and old boyfriends, giggling as she remembered breaking the nuns' many rules. The girls shared small rooms where they slept two or three to a bed, arms sprawled across shoulders, the older girls squeezing in late at night when they came home from a long evening of dancing in high heeled shoes, smelling of cigarettes, sweat, and gin.

A car pulled up out front and honked twice. Blowing a kiss to Pauline and Lucille, Agnes said, "Don't wait up," and left in a whirl of perfume and rustling stockings.

Later that evening, when the younger children were in bed, Pauline sat with Paul and Maude on the front porch. The radio was turned low in the background and they talked quietly in the dark, while Maude fanned her face with an old newspaper. The younger kids were asleep, worn out from a long day of play. After dinner they had shared a cake that Maude baked from scratch, a small indulgence for her forty-second birthday. They sat contentedly, grateful for any wisp of air.

The street in front of their house was also quiet. The neighbors were inside or sitting on their front porches, hoping for a passing breeze. Paul turned to look at the sound of a car approaching, an event on this lethargic evening. That it was a police car was of even greater interest, at least until it pulled up outside their house, in front of their own porch, as if the officer had business somewhere in their neighborhood. *Oh dear God, I hope the neighbors are all right,* was Maude's silent prayer, not once thinking that he could be coming toward her own door.

He climbed from his car and peered through the dusk at the surrounding houses. Paul called out to him, asking if there was something he could help him find. "I'm looking for Paul Dion," the man said, taking a step forward. "You found him," Paul said, moving to the front door of the porch. The man came forward then, taking off his hat as he walked, his face somber, his eyes turned down. Watching him, Maude placed her hand over her heart, her eyes fixed on the man's face.

"Mr. Dion, I'm sorry to have to tell you that your daughter, Agnes Dion . . ." but the words refused to come clear to Maude, they fused together in a blend of shock, horror, and grief. She heard fragments, phrases like "sharp curve" and "too fast," mixed with other words whose finality was beyond her ability to absorb. She nodded her head when Paul placed his hat on his head and left with the policeman. Pauline had already run upstairs to tell her sister, Lucille, and to sit with the younger kids in case they woke up. Maude moved slowly to the kitchen, where she stood at the sink, forgetting what had brought her there. She simply stared at nothing, her mind blessedly empty except for the white shock of news that only became real when she buried her daughter Agnes on Norma's sixth birthday, three days later.

Among her clothes and personal things, Maude found a bundle of letters that she had written to Agnes at St. Francis. Agnes had saved four years of letters from her family and friends, all of them folded neatly inside their original envelopes. The last one, written just before her accident, was by a jilted boyfriend who implored her to slow down.

In the days that followed, a heavy silence settled on the house. It was not possible that Agnes was gone, the girl who always looked out for her younger sisters at St. Francis, whose lively personality drew others to her so easily. She had spent most of her life away at St. Francis, and now that absence was permanent, as if she was still at school and would not come home again. There was little left to remind them of Agnes's short life except a framed photograph on the table.

A week after the funeral, Paul walked into the upstairs bedroom where Pauline and Lucille were sitting on the bed. Paul stood there for a moment without speaking, his hands in his pockets, an old man at forty-four, already stoop shouldered, his thinning hair disheveled. With his eyes on the floor, he said, "I'll be driving you two down to Holy Rosary tomorrow. Get your things together." He looked at them both briefly, his eyes filled with such sorrow that they said nothing at all in response to this news. Paul turned and walked slowly down the stairs. He called out to Maude and they heard the front door slam as he left for his evening visit to the corner tavern.

Pauline leaned over to Lucille and said, "I'm glad you're coming with me. It's not so bad, you'll see." Lucille nodded, numbly accepting that it was her turn to leave for boarding school. She knew that there was no work, that her family was barely able to feed all of them. Lucille was already ten years old, much older than her sisters were when they left for boarding school the first time.

In the morning Lucille and Pauline climbed silently into the backseat of their uncle's car. Each girl carried a bag with underclothes and socks. The school would provide them with the pinafores that all female students were required to wear. As they drove away, Lucille and Pauline turned to wave goodbye to their mother, still standing in front of the house with the baby, Sonny, waving back.

For the next four years, Lucille and Pauline lived at Holy Rosary from September through the following June. They did not come home for Christmas, nor did their family have the money to visit them. If they complained, Maude told them, "Hush, girls, you're lucky to have food and a place to live. There's a lot of white children who don't even have that."

9 *A Visit Home*

APRIL 1940
Holy Rosary Mission School, South Dakota

Lucille waited on the front steps of the Holy Rosary church, where the priests held Mass each morning, one foot tapping on the sidewalk while she chewed the raw end of a hangnail. She was impatient to be off for a day of unexpected pleasure. Two tall pine trees, faded from drought and twisted by South Dakota's fierce blizzard winds, cast a thin shadow where she sat huddled in her sweater against the cool April air. She was waiting for Father Zimmerman to finish his work in the church office. He had promised to drive her to Rapid City for a surprise visit to her family.

"Just a minute more, Lucille," Father Zimmerman called out, his lean face appearing just outside the church door. "And then we'll be off to see your folks."

"Thank you, Father," was her polite reply, although he had already disappeared within the shadow of the church entrance. She smoothed the skirt of her pinafore across thin legs, adjusted cotton socks that pinched a bit across the toes. She had not seen her parents or her sisters and brother in nearly eight months. It was early in the spring of 1940 and Lucille was in the eighth grade.

The school, with its several large dormitories and imposing church, was built in a shallow valley north of the town of Pine Ridge. In the late 1800s, Red Cloud, chief of the Oglala Sioux, shared Spotted Tail's belief that war with whites was hopeless. He asked the government to allow the Jesuit Blackrobes to minister on the Pine Ridge reservation, wanting his people to learn English while maintaining Lakota traditions. The Catholic Church

83

hoped to win a few new converts, and the government hoped that their efforts would result in further assimilating Indians through education. By 1940, the school had added the girls' dormitory, Red Cloud Hall, and a gymnasium. Students worked in the large gardens, where they grew potatoes and other vegetables, helped make bread in the bakery, and learned to raise cattle at a nearby ranch for the meat used in the school's meals.

Lucille lived next door to the church in a large dormitory with fifty beds lined up head to foot and separated by narrow aisles. A box at the foot of her bed held a change of clothes, letters from home, and a special bar of soap shaped like a rose. This was her one treasure, a gift sent by her mother for her birthday.

Earlier that morning she had been clearing dishes after breakfast when Father Zimmerman stopped at her table. "I've got business in Rapid City today, Lucille. Would you like a visit home?" His smile creased deep lines at the corners of his eyes as he waited for her answer.

"Oh yes, Father, I would like that very much," she had said. School had become so lonely after Pauline had been sent home with a serious ear infection that required surgery. Lucille had a close friend, Esther Black Elk, but no one could take her sister's place. Pauline was her confidante and playmate, someone who knew how much it hurt when the full-blood girls teased them, calling them *wasichus* for their light skin. Pauline always said, "Oh, the heck with them," as if what they said didn't matter.

Rapid City was only a three-hour drive from Holy Rosary, but her parents could not afford to travel, so Lucille thought there was no hope of a visit before the summer break. Students seldom went home for holidays unless their relatives could pick them up and drive them home. At Christmas, Maude sent Lucille a card signed with love from all the family. After Mass Lucille had been handed a piece of hard candy by a Franciscan Sister, the one with kind eyes and a young smile. She knew that many of her students came to Holy Rosary because their families could not afford to feed them at home.

"Please hurry, Father, please." Lucille whispered these words like a prayer, hoping they would hurry him up. She could see the sun moving higher overhead. If they left soon, she might be home in time for dinner. Her mother's cooking was a miracle after the bland diet they lived on at school: boiled potatoes with stringy bits of meat for supper, and hot cereal every single morning after Mass.

Lucille couldn't wait to see how big Darlene and Norma and especially her baby brother, Sonny, who was almost six, had grown. Maybe she would even see Pauline. She hoped her dad was sitting on the front steps, wearing his favorite hat, the one that made him look like a cowboy. He would be so surprised to see Father Zimmerman's old car come puffing up to the curb, especially when she jumped out as soon as the tires stopped moving. She had grown since he had last seen her, her long skinny legs earning her the nickname of "Sticks."

She guessed that nothing much had changed in the house since she left last fall. The same worn-out couch in the living room, still sagging in the middle where the springs were broken. Her mother's handmade curtains, faded from years of sun, still hanging in the window. Since they moved a lot, there was not much else besides a table and a few chairs. Her mother said there was no sense unpacking a lot of stuff only to move it again in a few months. And sometimes they had to move quick, when the rent was too far behind to ever catch up. But they always kept a picture of her sister Agnes on the table.

But Lucille would not even see her family if Father Zimmerman didn't finish his work soon. She stood up, impatient and cold, and looked again for his car to come chugging around the corner. She could see nothing but the placid face on the statue of the saint who stood near the road that led back to the world, to a precious few hours of freedom. At least she was allowed to wait outside rather than behind a locked door guarded by a nun with a large set of keys hanging from her waist.

Solitude was even more precious than the butter the nuns doled out, one small pat for each student. Pauline used to steal extra butter when the nun turned away and hide it under the table. School was easier then, with Pauline's lively humor a welcome relief from the regimented schedule. Now Lucille had to wait for the infrequent letters written when her mother or sisters had time, and she counted the days until the summer break would begin.

Tires crunched gravel and the long hood of the mission's official car rolled around the corner of the building, the wind blowing Father Zimmerman's hair into his eyes. He wasn't a bad-looking man, especially for a priest. His long black skirt, however, saved him from seeming too handsome in the eyes of his female students. He was also a bit stooped around the shoulders from all the long hours of bending his tall frame to hear the confessions that were whispered to him. Years later, his kind heart and long service among the Lakota Indians earned him the name of Wanblee Wankatuya, or High Eagle.

The car pulled in front of the curb, its engine clattering, a puff of smoke sighing from a tail pipe that hung dangerously near the road. Father Zimmerman leaned across the seat and threw the door open for Lucille to climb in.

Father Joseph Zimmerman

"It's a fine day for a drive," he said, squinting at the clear sky overhead. Barely a cloud to be seen, just the slow circle of a golden-tailed hawk riding the wind that blew steadily from the southwest, promising an early spring. A welcome sign after the massive blizzard a few weeks earlier, which had paralyzed the area for several days.

They turned north, choosing a direct route that ran alongside the eastern edge of the Black Hills. It was hard to talk over the noise of the engine and the whistle of the wind against the windows. Lucille leaned her head back against the seat and closed her eyes, feeling the warmth of the sun on her right leg and arm. She was tired from waking up each morning at five to the sound of a nun moving quietly down the aisles between the beds, saying, "Good morning, girls. Time for Mass."

Lucille fell asleep to the steady drone of the engine. When she woke an hour later they had already passed the invisible border that marked the edge of the reservation. Holy Rosary sat in the middle of wide-open land that wasn't much good for anything except grazing a few cattle on the stubby grass that covered the hills. Some years there was enough rain to grow a few acres of corn. Other years the sun baked the ground so hard that any rain just ran off, cutting new ravines between the hills. That's where the trees tended to grow, waiting for the water that rushed past.

The Black Hills loomed on the horizon, the pine trees growing so close together that they looked black from a distance.

"How much longer?" Lucille asked, even though she knew the answer too well.

"I'd like to say it was just over the next hill, but then I'd be needing to find confession myself," Father Zimmerman replied. "Let's just say we've got another hour to admire God's handiwork in these hills. Wasn't he a fine craftsman, Lucille?"

Lucille nodded and turned her head toward the window, dutifully admiring the view while hoping to discourage any further pious thoughts from the Father. The hour crept past and suddenly she could see the houses and buildings that formed the outer edge of Rapid City. This was still a cowboy town, a place where men came to trade cattle and to spend a few hours swapping stories in the bars. In 1940, Rapid City was also a place of deep hostility and racial tension between whites and Indians. Large signs in the windows of nightclubs and bars declared "No Indians Allowed." If Lucille and her sisters were sometimes teased by the full bloods at school as *wasichus*, when they came home they were called names like "squaw" or "chief." But she was still excited to see familiar landmarks as they drove past the building where Black Hills gold was turned into jewelry and past the Sioux museum and finally turned toward the part of town where the Indians and the mixed bloods and the people with no money lived.

They turned down Lucille's street and Father Zimmerman carefully parked the car on the side of the road. She flung open her door as soon as he stopped. She ran across the road, her heart beating hard against her chest, but then she slowed down, almost as if hesitating. There was something about the house that was different. It was the windows, maybe, that seemed blank and cold, as if the life had gone out of them. The screen door slapped gently on its loose hinge as she called out, "Mom? Dad? I'm home!"

Lucille pushed open the front door. She took several steps inside and stood very still, hardly breathing, as she turned her head to look carefully around the room. There was the couch in its place, the braid rug on the floor, but the air was flat, as if the house had been closed up for some time. As she turned toward the front window she felt her skin grow cold. Agnes's picture was missing, its empty place exposed in the layer of dust on the table. Her family was gone.

10 *The American Dream*

I stopped by my parents' house before work one morning to drop off the cooler that my daughter and I had borrowed on our trip to the Black Hills in South Dakota. It was almost 9:00 AM, too early for the small Minneapolis theater where I worked, but late enough that I knew my mother would be sitting alone at the kitchen table, drinking instant Folgers and reading the paper. My dad, long since retired from Sears, was still asleep.

The garage door was open, a sign that my mother was expecting me. Squeezing around the Oldsmobile, I stacked the cooler in the corner and stood for a moment in the dim light, appreciating how little this house changed from one year to the next. My parents had lived in this three-bedroom rambler for thirty-six years, almost my entire life, surrounded for decades by the same families. The long backyard where we played kick-the-can was now filled with mature lilac bushes and tall trees, all planted by my dad after work.

I walked through the family room on my way to the kitchen, passing a portrait of Spotted Tail, a gift to my mother from one of my brothers. It hung in a room filled with bargain furniture from Sears outlet stores and old wicker chairs that had belonged to my Swedish grandparents.

My mother offered me a cup of coffee, bracing one hand on the edge of the table as if she meant to get up. I grabbed the kettle and told her to save her legs.

"How was your trip?" she asked.

"Hot," I said. "Hot and a lot of miles. Jodi told me she never wants to go on another road trip with me again."

My mother laughed. "You're just like your dad," she said. "He won't even stop to fix a sandwich." Our family has a well-earned reputation as "road warriors," jumping in the car on impulse and driving for days with little rest.

She offered me a sweet roll covered in white icing. "Is this the diabetic variety?" I asked, knowing her love of forbidden sweets despite the diabetes that runs through our family.

No reply. She cut off a wedge and placed it on her napkin.

We sat without speaking for a few minutes, my mother in her usual chair near the toaster and the phone. She was sixty-five, but her hair was still dark, streaked lightly with gray around her face. She liked to get up early in the morning, before my dad, and sit quietly with her coffee, her Jungle Pink fingernails a bright contrast to her white cup. Like all of her sisters, she has remained a beautiful woman as she grows older, although I liked to remind her that the family parakeet once found her nose, with its high ridge, a convenient landing place. She just tells me to look in the mirror.

My mother, as always, was turned toward the window so she could watch the sparrows at the feeder in the front yard. Her eyes were softened with age, but they still commanded obedience from her grandchildren with a single look, just as they did from her own children. She never raised her voice with us, instead using silence like a cattle prod, nudging us to behave. I once told her an outright lie while she stood at the stove, stirring a pot of homemade spaghetti for dinner. I waited for her to reply, to either accept my version of the truth or deny it, so that I could defend myself. She said nothing, continuing to stir the spaghetti with a slow circle of her wood spoon. Finally, my conscience had no choice but to look inward. I never lied to her again.

Every morning when I was growing up, after my dad left for work and the breakfast dishes were done, she settled in her chair for a long talk with her sister Pauline. When we came home from school, she was chopping vegetables at the counter for a hot dish, her fingers always smelling faintly of onions. She had little advice to offer us as we grew up in the tumultuous 1960s, but her presence was an unquestioned constant in our lives. Nor did she treat any of her kids as a favorite, instead letting us know, without saying it, that she cherished each one of us as special in our own way. No matter how far we wandered, she would be waiting in her chair at the kitchen table when we returned, always ready to hear news from the world outside her window.

"Have you been to Wounded Knee?" I asked.

She shook her head.

"I took Jodi there. That's a hard place to visit."

"You sure know how to have a good time," she said. "I don't think I'd go on a road trip with you either."

We both laughed.

"We also stopped at Holy Rosary," I continued. "But it was closed up, so we didn't get to see anything."

My mother listened but said nothing. That part of her life was over, done with.

"We tried to camp at Fort Ridgely on our way home," I continued, breaking the silence. "It's a beautiful park. We set up our tent in the afternoon, but something didn't feel right, like the air was heavy, hard to breathe. We threw everything in the back of the car and drove the rest of the way home that night."

The brochure had described it as a heavily wooded, historic site for camping, complete with a nine-hole golf course and hiking trails. We felt uncomfortable from the moment we drove in. I thought we were just overtired from the long drive and the heat.

Before I left, I carried a stack of folded laundry up from the basement to my mother's bedroom. When my sister Sue and I shared that small room, it was decorated with gilt-edged dressers and matching pink bedspreads. Our younger brothers, Dave and Randy, shared bunk beds in an even smaller room across the hall. The eldest, Dick, moved downstairs to his own private lair in our basement as a teenager.

The room was still pink, my mother's favorite color. A rosary hung from one corner of her dressing table, the only reminder that she had been raised Catholic. She had never attended a

Catholic church while we were growing up, preferring, she said, to keep her spiritual business private.

In the room next door, my father slept deeply, a soft snore escaping into the hallway. He had grown up in Rush City, a town built by Swedish Lutherans, where my grandparents had lived all of their lives. After watching his father, Charlie, a grocery merchant, lose everything during the Depression, Chuck focused his sharp intelligence on the best way to "move the merchandise" as the manager for Sears, Roebuck's many outlet stores. He became a legend in the retail business, as much for his brusque nature as for his record-setting sales figures. He told us stories of his prowess—how 20,000 leisure suits were left unsold until he set a come-hither price and merchandised them so effectively that 20,000 people believed they should own one.

"It's all in how you sell yourself," he often reminded us, his blue eyes pinning each one of us briefly, insisting that we understand the importance of competition, of winning.

His mother, Alpha, was the tender-hearted daughter of a Lutheran minister who believed in good works but could not tolerate Catholics. Chuck was also a passionate, bible-reading Lutheran, but he offered my mother the Presbyterian Church as a compromise for raising their children. She agreed, and we attended until we became old enough to refuse.

I set my mother's laundry on her dresser near a thin stack of old photographs that were pinned together with a paper clip. The top photo had been taken during a play at Holy Rosary. My mother and her closest sister, Pauline, wore traditional buckskin dresses for their roles as "squaws." Their long, dark hair had been braided and held in place with beaded headbands. A young priest stood at the end of one row of students. Many of them appeared to be mixed bloods.

The photograph was one of the few reminders of my mother's Lakota heritage. She did not speak the language, never made fry bread, never asked that we attend a powwow, rarely mentioned her relatives still living in Mendota or South Dakota. Occasionally she would get a small check in the mail as payment for reservation land that had been leased in Nebraska or South Dakota. Her silence meant that we learned about Indians by watching the Lone Ranger and Tonto on television.

But one morning, on a day much like this one, hot and bright and humid, she had surprised me. I was about eleven years old, dawdling in the garage out of curiosity, or "nose trouble" as my mother called it, waiting for the Salvation Army truck to arrive. Our summer days were so placid and uneventful that the arrival of a big truck to carry away a donated couch was an event.

I was the first to see the truck backing into our driveway. I knew that curtains would be pushed open all along our street as the neighbor women craned their necks to see what was going on at the Wilson house. I stood unnoticed in the corner as two burly Indian men climbed out of the truck and walked into the garage. My mother came out the side door, a cardigan sweater thrown over her shoulders. She looked elegant even in the old slacks she wore while she cleaned. When she saw the men she smiled and said, "*Han kola!*" *Hello friend* in Lakota. They looked as surprised as I felt. One of the men nodded his head and returned the greeting.

Pageant at Holy Rosary Mission School, 1930s. Lucille, third row up, third girl from left; Pauline, second row up, fifth girl from left

Up until that moment, I thought my mother was the same as all the other mothers in the neighborhood. I knew about Rosebud and Holy Rosary, but they weren't real to me. My mother wore her hair cut short, drove my brothers to baseball practice in the station wagon, and showed up for parent-teacher conferences in a mom-style outfit. Standing in the garage that morning was the first time I realized she was different, not just from the neighbors, but from me.

I set the photograph back on the dresser, smoothing the delicate cloth that my grandfather Paul Dion had embroidered. From the window I could see the long row of houses that lined our street, most of them built in the 1950s, when Golden Valley was expanding as fast as people could buy up farmland. Our yard, once cow pasture, was surrounded by families raising young children. We ran freely through each other's yards, stole apples from the neighbor's tree, and played with cattails we picked at a nearby swamp. Sometimes we swapped stories that we heard from our parents, asking, "What are you?" referring to our ancestors' country of origin. My best friend next door was English and Danish, the family across the street was Finnish, and two doors down lived a woman from Scotland. We were part Indian, French, and Swedish.

Each day we rode a bus to school where everyone was white except for two kids who had been adopted into an Asian family. Our neighbors worried about "blockbusting," the fear that a non-white family moving into the neighborhood would drive down real-estate prices. The suburbs were a bastion of conservative whites, and my mother, a non-graduate from the Holy Rosary Mission School on the Pine Ridge reservation, lived in their midst.

Standing in my mother's room, with the dust from Pine Ridge still fresh on my car, I wondered what difference it made, if any, knowing my family history. The whole point of the suburbs was that we were safe, finally—safe from nameless, faceless dangers that lurked within those memories. If my mother was right, then it was time to lay down the relics of the past, keeping only a few photographs to remind us of how far we had come.

11 *Leap of Faith*

Halfway between Rapid City and the eastern border of South Dakota, the land flattens out as it leaves behind the hard, carved rockscape of the Badlands. The near mountains of the Black Hills turn to an endless expanse of dry plains that blend into prairie near the Missouri River. The slow movement of a glacier thousands of years earlier had split the state of South Dakota into two distinct regions: plains to the west of the Missouri and prairie to the east.

Late in March 1940, a few weeks before Lucille's ill-fated trip home, a rusted car near the end of its useful life appeared on the horizon, heading east. The afternoon was cold and gray, with a thick band of dark clouds forming in the sky to the west. A sharp wind blew across the snow-covered fields, piling snow in fresh drifts against the fence lines that stretched for miles. The air was heavy with moisture that warned of a storm on its way.

Staring straight ahead as the first few flakes of snow began to swirl across the hood of the car, Paul Dion resisted the temptation to look in his rearview mirror at the clouds moving steadily toward them. He knew it was foolish to try and outrun a South Dakota blizzard. Especially with his wife and four of his children in the car. Yet he drove on as fast as he dared, his hands white-knuckled on the steering wheel.

Maude sat next to Paul in the front seat. Her hands were folded together in her lap, her thin gloves intertwined for warmth. None of them was dressed for a blizzard. Maude wore a wool dress but her legs were bare except for her stockings and long coat. She turned her collar up around her neck, her fingers smoothing the frayed edge closer to her face. She, too, felt the clouds pressing behind them. But she knew what drove her husband to keep moving east, and she said nothing. Her only boy, Sonny, already six but always the baby with seven older sisters, slept between them.

Three girls huddled together in the backseat, their legs pressed close for warmth. The oldest girl, Pauline, wrapped her arms around her much younger sisters. Nine-year-old Norma and the youngest girl, Darlene, barely seven, leaned against Pauline's shoulders and slept. Darlene's curly head dropped forward but just as suddenly she woke up, her brown eyes fixed on Pauline's face. "Where are we going?" she asked. "To Grandma's house," Pauline whispered, revealing all that she knew of the reason for this unexpected trip.

Earlier that morning, Pauline had been upstairs in her room when she heard the front door bang open and her father's agitated voice call out. Recent surgery on her ear had kept her home from Holy Rosary while she recuperated, leaving her closest sister, Lucille, at school without her. She missed Lucille, missed her friends at school, too, although it was nice to sleep late in the morning. But the sound of her father's voice rising clear up the stairs was enough to rouse Pauline immediately. She was the mother hen of the other girls, and she liked to know what was going on.

Maude was in the kitchen washing the breakfast dishes when she heard Paul call her name. "Dear Lord," she said under her breath, "what's happened now?" Drying her hands on the counter rag, she hurried to the living room, where Paul was unbuttoning his coat in fumbling haste.

Pauline came quickly down the stairs, her face alight with curiosity.

"What is it, Paul, what's happened?" Maude asked, already fearing bad news. Lucille was away at school and the rent was so far behind that she hid from every knock at the front door. Ever since Agnes's death, she knew that only bad news came suddenly.

"I sold it, Maude. Sold the machine this morning. There's still time to get out before the storm hits." Paul strode to the front window and looked out, as if to prove to himself that the clouds already gathering that morning were not yet a threat. He knew what they were saying on the radio, had heard it while he was in town. There was no mistaking the fearful thrill in the announcer's voice as he predicted one of the winter's worst storms headed their way, folks. Time to lay in provisions, round up the cattle, keep your children close to home. Yes, sir, this would be a blizzard to remember.

But there were some things worse than storms. There was the awful gnawing anxiety of not working, of standing in lines waiting for an inadequate relief check that didn't come close to paying their bills. On top of that they had Pauline's doctor bills, but what choice do you have, the doctor said she might lose her hearing otherwise. He would work if he could find any, work damn hard despite the pain in his joints, the worn-out feeling that never left his bones, especially after his car accident a few years earlier, when he had been run over in front of his house. The car backed up to see what it had hit, running over him twice and leaving a tire imprint on his back. After three months in the hospital, he had come home, but he never felt the same after that.

"I don't know, Paul. This is all kind of sudden," Maude said, still wiping her hands on her apron in absentminded worry. Paul was already dragging from the closet an old, travel-worn trunk that had moved their family many times beyond the reach of persistent landlords. He came close to Maude then and shoved his hand deep in the baggy pocket of his pants. His fingers emerged clutching a thick roll of bills, more money than they'd seen in years.

"This is it, Maude, our ticket out of this hellhole." He shook it at her gently and went back to the trunk. It was Maude who had once described Rapid City as the "asshole of the nation," and she knew exactly how he felt. They would never be anything but white trash while they lived here, just down-on-their-luck, mixed-blood white trash who were unwelcome in either the white or the Indian world. She knew her daughters had to listen to names thrown at them, words like "squaw" or "chief" made ugly by the ignorant hate in people's voices. Paul knew what it was like to be sitting in a bar and hear the owner ask an Indian to leave, as it was illegal for Indians to be served alcohol. Paul's light skin and his silence paid for his privilege of sitting there. He never mentioned the Rosebud reservation, where he was enrolled, nor the lease payments from allotment land that helped them survive. He had learned silence when he realized that Indians were not hired first when a crew was needed and that his neighbors knew nothing but the stereotype of drunken Indians.

Back when Paul was recuperating from his car accident, he and Maude had talked about moving to Minneapolis, the great golden mecca to the east where work was rumored to be plentiful. Maude's mother, Jenny LaCroix, had moved back to Mendota, where she was born. Her infrequent letters talked of green gardens and new jobs, while South Dakota roasted on a double spit of drought and heat. Cattle were shipped by the thousands to nearby states, while fields of corn slowly burned in the sun. The land grew so parched that it simply lifted up, swirled into thick clouds of dust that blew across the state in "black blizzards." No travel advised, visibility limited to just a few feet. In the morning, barns had been buried beneath the weight of a neighbor's field, tractors had disappeared, dirt had piled up under the eaves of a house. They woke with a film of dust lining the insides of their mouths, filling their eyes, covering every horizontal surface.

It was a dream that they would ever have enough money for food and rent, much less to drive across the state and start again. When the cardboard wears out in a patched shoe, only to be replaced with more cardboard, it's hard to find the money for a car and gas. But parents feel the weight of responsibility for their children, and it was a man's job, and his pride, to support his family. It was a miracle, then, a thank-God-in-heaven moment, when Paul's brother-in-law, Oliver LaCroix, took him aside one afternoon. Oliver worked at the Sioux Sanitarium, and he knew when equipment was sometimes thrown away. He also knew that Paul was desperate for money.

Without stumbling over the legality of taking discarded equipment, Paul arranged to meet Oliver at the sanitarium the next morning as soon as it was light. Oliver worked as a maintenance man, so it was easy for him to borrow a truck and back it close to where he had seen an old laundry machine in good condition. Oliver took hold of one side of the machine, while Paul gripped the other. Paul was not a small man, but his body had lost strength after the accident. The machine offered the hope of salvation, however, and like a sinner who sees the possibility of redemption, he was rejuvenated.

With Oliver lifting hard on his side, Paul pushed against his body's weakness, feeling his old determination rise with the adrenalin now pumping into his blood. His face darkened as he strained, but his muscles thought first to resist this sudden effort. He groaned as he felt the weight slipping toward him, threatening to crush him, just as these long years of poverty had pressed his pride into the dirt, forcing him to move his family over and over. All the rage he had kept tamped down under a soft voice and gentle manner spilled out in a moan that gathered low in his chest, his voice rising in fierce hunger for this last bit of hope. His strength surged, the machine lifted all at once and settled into the back of the truck with a solid, reassuring thud.

They drove straight into town, where they sold the machine to a man with sense enough not to ask too much about where it came from. The machine might have been thrown away, but Paul was not about to call attention to the cash cow that the state had missed. He was far too afraid they would find a way to reclaim his windfall. For this was truly Paul's winning lottery ticket, his fastest horse, the one prayer his God had seen fit to answer.

On the way home, Paul bought a car from a man he trusted, paying his price in cash without question. While they counted out the money, the radio broadcast news of the storm heading their way, carrying untold inches of snow, straight-line winds, temperatures that would freeze flesh in minutes. Paul knew it was insanity to think of leaving, yet it felt like suicide to stay. Surely the landlord would hear of Paul's sudden cash and demand his share. Surely the doctor would come running for the overdue payment on Pauline's bills. And as surely as this storm was headed their way, if they didn't beat it out of town, they would have no money left to make this move.

Maude knew this as well as Paul, and she did not argue with his plan to leave immediately. As they waited for the younger kids to come home for lunch, they threw clothes into the trunk, along with a few pots and pans, extra blankets. Maude sent Pauline down to Oliver, Jr.'s house to say they were leaving. Pauline came back carrying a loaf of bread, her eyes sparkling with excitement from her role as the messenger with a dramatic story to tell. If Maude and Paul thought of their daughter Lucille at all, it was only with a sense of relief that she was taken care of. They would write, later, after the family was settled, and send for her when there was money.

Now Paul drove with the single-minded purpose of a man possessed. He spoke rarely, accustomed to steering the family's course with little explanation. They had moved often enough that even this change did not inspire many questions. Maude stared straight ahead at the fading light of her last afternoon in South Dakota. She left behind two daughters, one at Holy Rosary and one in the Catholic cemetery just outside Rapid City. She would miss her brother. She preferred not to think about what might lie ahead, knowing only that it would be difficult. They were driving blindly toward her mother's small house in Mendota, where they might at best stay a night or two. The money would disappear like rain in a South Dakota summer. There was nothing she could do but wait.

12 *Starting Over*

The small town of Mendota, *Mdo-te*, or "Meeting of the Waters," is nestled in the hills and valleys that surround the bluffs where the Mississippi and Minnesota rivers meet. On a blustery, gray morning, Jenny Felix LaCroix stood on the stoop of her small house looking out at the western sky. She pressed her lips tightly together at the bruised color of the clouds, her arms folded against the sharp wind that pulled at her shawl. Shaking her head, she mumbled to herself in French, "Someone is coming home."

She raised her head as if to sniff the air, closing her eyes to feel what stories the wind carried. She felt in her bones the pressure of the storm that loomed on the horizon, but there was more in this wind than just weather. "Ah, she rides the storm. *Pauvre fille.*" Still shaking her head at the impulsive ways of her children, she pulled at the door, forcing it open against the wind.

"Marie, Marie, come quickly," she called out. Her youngest daughter was upstairs, cleaning and sorting old boxes in the attic. Marie climbed the hill between their houses almost every day to check on her seventy-four-year-old mother, despite Jenny's surprisingly good health. Now Marie came hurrying down the short flight of stairs, wiping a cobweb from the front of her sweater. She had her mother's dark hair and wide smile.

"What is it, Mama, what is so urgent?" This was said patiently, without the edge of irritation that sometimes rises between a daughter and a feisty, aging mother.

Jenny's forceful personality had not faded as her hair turned

Jenny LaCroix's house (above) and her daughter Marie's garage (facing page) at Mendota

gray. It had been thirty-three years since the death of her husband, Oliver LaCroix, Sr., while her nine children were still young. Raising a family alone, even with the help of many relatives, trimmed all the fat from a woman's soul.

Jenny was already peering into the bin that held flour, measuring with her eye how many loaves she might bake that afternoon. Two, maybe three. Pulling her large mixing bowl from the cupboard, she spoke over her shoulder.

"They're coming, they'll be here tonight, maybe in the morning. Run and tell your husband that we'll need his garage. Sweep it out, light the wood stove, gather all the blankets you can spare." Jenny fired her instructions to Marie, organizing her thoughts as she spoke. She could count on Ted, he was as much her son as one of her own children. "I don't know how many," she added, answering one of Marie's as yet unasked questions.

"But who, Mama, who is coming? And how do you know?" asked Marie, certain that no one had been to town for the mail or had stopped to tell her mother in person.

"Maude is coming," Jenny said, her attention already focused on the handful of lard she was squeezing through the flour with her fingers. "I just know." She spoke no more, concentrating now on the task at hand. Feeling Marie's silent questions behind her, she turned her head and said sharply, "Go, girl, the storm's not waiting for you."

She heard the door slam as Marie left. In the silence that followed, broken only by the slap of the dough as she turned it on the board, Jenny wondered briefly at her daughter's sudden appearance. Why now, in this storm? She thanked God they had somehow found the money to leave, never mind how. The little she had heard of South Dakota was not good, even though things seemed to be getting better elsewhere. Too many people were still on relief, and too much anger still walked the streets with guns and cowboy attitudes. There would be time enough to talk later. The last few letters she'd had from Maude could not hide her grief and worry. Well, it seemed like everybody had a hard story behind them.

Jenny wondered how many children would be coming. Certainly the little ones, Darlene and Norma, and the baby, Sonny, who was probably crawling by now, at least. The two oldest girls were married, and the others were most likely still in school. She looked at her cramped living room with a critical eye. Grabbing the broom, she swept a small pile of crumbs to the middle of the floor. *If they come late,* she thought, *they might just as easily sleep here tonight. Maude and Paul can use my room and the children can sleep on the floor. I can stay with Marie or Clarence, or even Lillian.* Her

three youngest children lived in the area. They were married, of course, and nobody had any money, but they would gladly share what they had.

She stopped sweeping and sighed, deeply, clear down to the back of her ribs, at the thought of seeing Maude again. Jenny never thought that Maude would leave South Dakota. She and her older brother, Oliver, Jr., had seemed fairly settled in Rapid City. Most of Jenny's kids had already returned to Mendota or close enough for her to visit easily. Why, you couldn't walk down the street without running into a LaCroix or a Felix. It was like the years when she was growing up in Mendota, long before her family had moved to the Santee reservation.

In the old days, before the 1862 war, Mendota had been a central gathering place for many tribes to meet for spring councils, to hold ceremonies and bury their dead on scaffolds. Mendota has always been sacred to Dakota people because of its location near the mouth of the Minnesota River. The area now called Pilot Knob was known as Oheyawahi, "a hill much visited," where the Dakota used to hold their medicine ceremony, the Wakan Wacipi.

Oheyawahi was also the place where the Mdewakanton and Wahpekute signed the treaty of 1851, which surrendered all of their land west of the Mississippi River. Back then a community of fur traders, Dakota people, mixed bloods, and settlers lived around the trading post where Henry Sibley, who had arrived in 1834, traded European goods with area tribes. Jenny's father, Peter Felix, had met his Ojibwe wife, Margaret Bellecourt, Ge-Shah-Day-Quay, when her parents came down from Mille Lacs and settled around Mendota, shortly before the war broke out at Lower Sioux.

When Jenny's parents married in 1860, Mendota was a rough settlement with frequent drinking and fighting. Jenny used to travel with her parents while her father looked for odd jobs. In the spring they tapped maple trees and made sugar to sell. One night a small band of Indians found them camping in a field. Her dad told Jenny and her mother to be quiet and stay hidden. He spoke French and Dakota and went out to talk to the Indians. They were angry and called Peter a half-breed and threatened to kill him. He managed to calm them down and they left.

Twenty years after Oliver, Sr., died at Santee, Jenny came home to Mendota in the late 1920s with her three youngest children, Clarence, Lillian, and Marie. It had been hard to return, at first, because they were all poor and no one had electricity or plumbing, but Jenny was content to be back on the land where she had grown up. They moved in with her sister, Lilly, and Jenny sold her beadwork, crocheting, and knitting. When she was able to get some money together, she bought a lot in Mendota from her son, Clarence, who was working for the railroad, and he built the little house that she lived in.

Even though quite a few of her relatives had left Mendota, sometimes for many years, the area seemed to pull many of them back home again. Jenny's youngest sister, Mary, had come back and married Frederic LaBatte. Lilly was married to Albert LeClair and sometimes came to visit with their grandson, Bob Brown. Jenny's uncle, Denis Felix, the old soldier from the 1862 Dakota War, had moved back and lived in Prior Lake until his death in 1928. Jenny's parents and her grandparents, Rosalie Frenier and Peter Felix, were buried in the cemetery behind St. Peter's Church.

Jenny swept the crumbs onto a piece of newspaper. She needed a good fire going in her stove if she wanted to bake this bread today. Maybe she could throw the old ashes in the outhouse, sweeten it up a bit. If Clarence stopped by after work, he could refill her wood box and carry in another pail of water from the rain bucket out front. She hoped he wouldn't head out to his cabin on Green Lake first. It was a great place for fishing, but she wasn't sure if he was still holding a grudge from the small misunderstanding they had had last year.

Clarence knew that Jenny loved to fish, and sometimes he picked her up on his way to his cabin. She had a big, beat-up black purse that she always took fishing with her. The purse was filled with old rags so she could wipe her hands after putting worms on the hook. Well, one day she caught a beautiful bass, the biggest one ever. She could practically taste it. Clarence must have seen her salivating because he told her straight out that she couldn't keep it, bass weren't in season. And if they got caught . . . There was silence for a while after that. Clarence was busy with his own line and she kept her back turned toward him. After a while, they headed back toward the dock. Everything would have worked out just fine if the damn purse hadn't started to flop around in the bottom of the boat. Clarence was mad at first, but then they had a good laugh about it.

Jenny leaned toward her stove, bending more stiffly than she would let on to any of her daughters, and shoved a few more sticks of wood into the already crackling fire. As soon as the flames died down to hot coals, she could place her bread in the oven. She looked out the window to see how much ice was covering the road. She wanted to walk down to Marie's house and check on the garage. Who knew how long Maude and her family would have to live there before they found work? She knew from Maude's letter that Paul was not a well man.

The road had a slight, icy sheen to it that she was reluctant to risk. Maybe one of the grandchildren had left a sled lying around the yard. She still knew how to ride one of those, and it certainly wouldn't be the first time she had come flying down the hill to Marie's house, much to Marie's concern. Or maybe she would just sit for a minute with a cup of cedar tea. The night would be long and eventful. "Ah, well," Jenny said under her breath, and then sighed deeply. It would be difficult, but that was life, wasn't it? You did what you had to do, and you made the best of it.

BOOK TWO

If you know what was taken away, then you can reclaim it.

DAVID LARSEN
Historian, Lower Sioux

13 *Corn Husks & Bun Time*

OCTOBER 1992
Richfield, Minnesota

About a year after my trip to Holy Rosary, I had lunch with Germaine Tremmel, a Lakota woman from Standing Rock, South Dakota, whom I had met at the theater where I worked as an arts administrator. She talked about the traumatic effect boarding schools had on Indian people. She said, "Someone needs to tell that story." I knew even then that it had to be written by someone who was raised within Dakota culture, who could speak from that perspective. I was not that person. But I could, instead, tell my own family's part in that larger story, provided I could persuade them to share it with me.

When my aunt Midge came to town for a month-long visit, I called my mother and asked to talk to her and her sisters as a group about their experience at boarding school. I expected resistance, knowing their generation often prefers to not dwell on the past, especially times that were hard or painful. To my surprise, they all agreed immediately, even my mother.

We met at Pauline's house in Richfield, where she had raised four children with her husband, Art Sandquist. Midge was visiting from Florida, where she had recently survived Hurricane Andrew. My mother stopped to pick up Florence, who lived alone in an apartment in Minneapolis and didn't drive. Except for Midge and Sonny, who had enlisted in the navy and then moved to Texas, most of the Dions had settled near the Twin Cities after moving here in 1940. All the Dion daughters married men of European descent who promised to be good providers.

Paul and Maude LaCroix Dion and their daughters, about 1952: left to right, Norma, Darlene, Florence, Pauline, Lucille, Midge, Margaret

After their wild ride from Rapid City to Mendota fifty-two years earlier, the Dions lived in Aunt Marie's single-car garage in Mendota for nearly a year: four kids, two adults, a couple of mattresses, blankets, a suitcase or two of clothing, and a wood stove. Finally, Paul was able to scrape together enough money to open a dry cleaning business, Sparkle Cleaners No. 2, near the University of Minnesota in Dinkytown. He and Maude moved to a big, run-down house in south Minneapolis, where they lived until he passed away from complications of diabetes in 1955. After Paul's death, Maude retired to a cabin on Medicine Lake until she died from cancer in 1962.

We had lunch first, of course—grilled hamburgers and decaffeinated coffee served in china cups in Pauline's meticulously decorated dining room. The women discussed their many grandchildren and their struggles with diabetes and breast cancer. After lunch, we carried our cups to the kitchen and arranged ourselves around a beautifully restored wood table that had belonged to Maude.

My mother and her sisters sat patiently waiting for whatever was to come next, still chatting happily with each other. I cleared my throat, fumbled with the buttons on the tape recorder. This is the step that stops many people from going any further in learning about their families, only to say later, when it's too late, that they wished they had listened to the stories their relatives tried to tell them. There is a deep hunger at work here, both to tell the stories and to hear them, yet few people will take the time to listen because it's not an easy thing to do. It's unnerving to pry into a family member's past, to accept the tacit admission that there was a life entirely separate from your relationship together, even to shoulder the family's unspoken legacy. To interview these women, especially my mother, I had to see them as strangers. Our conversation that afternoon, and their willingness to share their lives, was a pivotal moment in my search for family stories.

Where to begin? Taking a deep breath, I asked them how they felt as kids, living in the mission schools. Surprisingly, my mother answered first. Sometimes it was hard to hear her over the more strident voices of her sisters.

"You didn't want to be there. If we had a choice, we wouldn't have gone. We wanted to be with our parents. They kept us when they could and used mission schools as a last resort."

All of them spoke at once, agreeing that it was a very lonely place to be as a child. Pauline said, "We had no choice, and we made the best of it."

The oldest sister, Midge, explained that it helped to have a sister at school. At seventy-two, Midge is short and wiry, with the raspy voice of a former smoker. The sisters were often

Paul Dion, Jr. (Sonny), who had enlisted in the navy, 1952

paired by age growing up, and Midge and Florence were sent to St. Francis in 1926, when Midge was six and Florence was five. They shared a bed because Florence was so homesick.

I asked why they went to St. Francis.

"Our dad went to school there. Him and his brothers," Midge said.

"There were nine boys in that family and they were all cowboys, cowpunchers. Until they grew up and got married and they all split." Florence could recall details as if they had occurred only yesterday. She sat at one end of the table with a bemused expression on her unlined face. She had an almost dreamy quality about her and wore a long strand of beads with her ruffled pink blouse. Later she recited the Catholic sign of the cross in Lakota for us.

Midge repeated my question. "You want to know why? Because it was free. It didn't cost nothing, in those days the government paid for it."

"I think they just couldn't stand us . . . that's all," Florence said

The Dion sisters, October 1992: left to right, Florence, Pauline, Midge, Lucille

in her soft voice. The sisters all laughed, but it was a theme that Florence repeated over the next two hours.

As I watched Midge flipping through pages of the St. Francis centennial album, I wondered, but did not ask, if my aunts knew the history of boarding schools. In the late 1800s, the government wanted to assimilate Indians as quickly as possible into white culture. Mission schools like St. Francis and Holy Rosary were set up by Jesuit priests and nuns. Indian children were removed from their culture at an early age so they would be raised with white values and skills. In the early decades, children were forcibly taken from their families, their hair was cut, and they were forbidden to speak their native language, as part of the plan to force Indians to "break away from the blanket."

Shortly after Midge and Florence started school in the 1920s, a long-overdue report identified boarding schools as the symbol of all the evils of the education program run by the Bureau of Indian Affairs. Children were malnourished, lacked adequate medical care, and lived in dangerously overcrowded conditions. The teaching staff was considered to be "grossly inadequate." Tuberculosis had reached epidemic proportions. While this was not my family's experience, some students suffered physical and emotional abuse, including rape and sodomy.

I asked what living in the dormitory was like. Pauline leaned forward on her elbows, her lively face gleaming as if she knew a dirty joke and couldn't wait to tell it. She wore bright colors and a hearing aid that peeked from a halo of permed hair around her face. A natural storyteller, Pauline is the hub of the family, the one who keeps in touch with the distant relatives. Growing up, she and Lucille were so close that they often said they were "joined at the hip." They still spend hours every day talking on the phone.

"We'd have these big corn-husking parties and we'd all gather corn when it was colder than heck," Pauline explained. "We would have these corn-husking feeds where all the kids would gather around the big pile of dried corn cobs. And the sewing room would prepare the mattresses out of ticking and they would be all ready except they would leave one end open to be stuffed with corn husks. And we stuffed the heck out of them because this was going to be our mattress for the coming year. And you never heard so much noise in all your life when they rolled over." And she laughed, which was the way most of her stories ended.

Midge spoke next, holding her cup carefully in her small, calloused hand. She seemed surprised at what she remembered, that somehow she had managed to forget how difficult those years had been. "Come to think of it, we sure didn't have much. We had these little boxes where we had our change of clothes and that's all we had. Everything we owned, we had one set of clothes we wore and then we had a clean set in the box with our number on it. That was all the belongings we had."

"Much like the prison system, I would imagine," Lucille said.

Pauline added, "That's always what I thought it was, a prison." Her optimistic attitude did not prevent her from recognizing the harsh conditions they had lived in.

The reason for all that security, Florence said, fingering the beads around her neck, was because of the kids who tried to run away. "The prairie storms are different, you know, there's no hills or anything to stop the wind. So when you get a snowstorm or it's icy cold out, some of these kids would be found kneeling and frozen to death. Like under a bridge or something, the kids that ran away. And there were a lot of them. They didn't want you going out in the storm."

Each morning they rose at five and attended Mass at six. "Then we marched to breakfast," Pauline said. "Oatmeal, and what, a bun. Single file, very regimented. Quiet. Never out of line." The resourceful girls, like Pauline, stole an extra pat of butter and hid it under the table. "And then you'd have an extra butter!" she crowed. "Unless it got really hot," Lucille quickly added, which sent the sisters into another round of laughter.

After breakfast, before classes started, they were each assigned to work details in the laundry, sewing, dining room, kitchen, or infirmary. Pauline said that when she was working on kitchen detail, there would often come a knock at the back door.

"The sister would say, 'Open the door.' Outside would be a wagon with a dog and an old Indian with his wife. She would come up to the door with her pail and her shawl and her moccasins and ask for food. It would often be very stormy weather and they were riding in this wagon. Who knows how many miles. We'd hand out the leftovers to whoever would come to the door. Many times there would be more than five or six people."

Each grade was assigned to a room where they would be instructed in arithmetic, English, history, and Latin in the higher grades. They also put on plays to raise money for the school.

After classes, they returned to their work details for an hour in the afternoon, learning to sew, crochet, and embroider. Then they were sent to the playroom where they waited for "bun time."

"We used to roast our apples against that big stove they had in the playroom," Florence said. "They had this huge playroom where about 150 kids played. They had a great big stove that looked like a furnace and they'd give us apples at four o'clock, that would be our little snack."

"Or we'd get a hot bun," Pauline said.

Holy Rosary Mission School basketball team, 1930s; Pauline Dion is to the right of Sister Adelaide.

Baths or showers were taken once a week, and Midge remembered "a big nun standing by the door when you went in to take your shower." Florence said she was scared the first time she used the flush toilets because she had only used the "outdoor biff" until then. The aunts all laughed and said to me, "See how good you have it?"

"This is depressing to think about all this stuff," Midge said, almost to herself.

"I was so young when I went there I think I kind of got used to it right away," Florence said. "I thought, well shoot, this is the way life is."

"I looked forward to the simplest things, like when you went home from school, getting a fresh loaf of bread and a new set of clothes to go home in," Midge said.

"Even on a holiday, at Christmas, you'd get an orange or an apple," Lucille recalled.

"Right! And a piece of hard candy. And I usually hated it," Pauline said, and she laughed.

I asked, "Did you go home for the holidays?" There was a chorus of no's. "I remember when we first started going to St. Francis," Midge said. "On holidays, on Easter, right out there where the museum is, that part used to be full of tents. The Indians would come and camp there and be with their families."

The girls who could go home for visits came back with homemade chokecherry jellies and wild grape jams to put on their bread at "bun time." Pauline said wistfully, "We never got any goodies because our parents never came."

By the 1930s, mission schools began acting as a stop-gap survival tool for families like the Dions, who were struggling to live through the Depression. The schools provided free room and board to Indian children who qualified with at least one-quarter blood quantum. Margaret, Agnes, Midge, Florence, Pauline, and Lucille were sent to boarding school, while the three youngest—Norma, Darlene, and Sonny—attended public school in Minneapolis. My mother's family depended on boarding schools to survive, changing schools whenever the family moved looking for work. Their mixed-blood status allowed them to move between two worlds, living on the reservation only when they attended school.

But for full-blood children, the experience was much harsher. Not only did they feel the same mix of loneliness and abandonment, they were also forbidden to speak their native language, and they had little experience with the regimented discipline enforced by the nuns and priests. They were the real target of the government's education policy, while my mother and her sisters were merely caught in the cross fire.

I asked if it was difficult for the girls who were raised in traditional Indian families to adjust to the school. Pauline agreed that it was, saying, "That's why I think they have so many problems now."

"We sat on the fence between white and Indian," Florence explained. "You can't really adjust to either one."

"Because you don't feel like you belong in either," Midge said.

"Right," Florence agreed. "What you do is you develop a sense of humor about it. Mostly the Indian was what bothered us because people would make us feel . . ."

"Inferior," Lucille said.

"I don't know," Pauline said. "The Indians were that way, too."

"The full bloods were after us and the whites were after us," Florence said.

"They looked down on the mixed bloods," Midge added.

"They called us *wasichus*," Pauline explained.

"And you'd go home and they'd call you 'squaw' so you didn't know what you were," Midge said.

I turned then to my mother, asking her if she stayed at Holy Rosary through the ninth grade.

"I'm not sure, but I think I went through the tenth grade. That's the last grade I was there. And that's the last I went to school," she said.

"Then you moved to Minneapolis?"

"Yeah. Our family was already out there," she replied. "You've heard me complain about that. Two years there. A solid two years at the mission." Her wedding ring tapped quietly against the side of her cup.

Midge turned and looked at her. "You? Without going home?" Lucille nodded her head.

"Oh, my," was all Midge could say.

"I didn't remember . . ." Pauline murmured.

"They had a mission ranch where they had cattle and horses. It was run by a white family. Because I was there at the mission . . ."

"Was anybody else there?" Midge asked.

"One other person. And so I went and worked at the ranch for the summer. And that was nice. You work in the kitchen and laundry and that kind of stuff. I could ride horses so, you know, it wasn't all bad," Lucille explained.

"How did it happen that you were the only one left?"

"Because I was at school when Dad sold the machine he got from Uncle Smoky. They just loaded everything up and took off. I had to wait until they could afford to send for me," Lucille said.

"That was no picnic going to that school," Midge said. "Especially for her, being left there."

"I was devastated," my mother said.

"I bet," Midge replied. "What were they going to do about you?"

"Well, they had a carload of people and kids and so they left and they were going to send for me," Lucille replied.

"Oh, you poor thing," Midge said softly, laying her hand for just a moment on my mother's arm.

Lucille tried to laugh and said, "Well, it was bad."

I asked how she finally found her family.

"I think they wrote then or, I don't know, if I called Aunt Mary. But things were tough, you know."

Across the table, Pauline reached for one of her photo albums, which lay in a pile for the sisters to look at. Thumbing through its pages, she stopped and turned it toward me. Pointing to a grainy, black-and-white photograph, she said, "That's Aunt

Marie's garage. There was a blizzard coming, so we left Rapid City in a big hurry. We lived there for a year while Cille was at Holy Rosary." Flipping a few more pages, she pointed to a dilapidated farm house. "That's Oliver LaCroix's place down on Santee. His land is leased now to the tribe, that's why we get those big checks in the mail."

"Wait a minute," Lucille said. "I don't think I got mine this year. All two bucks of it." They shook their heads at the folly of the government's land system.

The conversation drifted on again, and across the table I could hear Midge saying as she pointed to a photograph of a nun in the St. Francis centennial album, "No wonder I've got beat-up knuckles today. This is the nun that used to do that."

Toward the end of the interview, when the talk was beginning to shift back toward grandchildren, I asked them what effect they thought mission schools had on their lives.

Pauline, the butter stealer who was always in trouble with the nuns for talking in line, said, "You know, I would do it over again. I think we were taught some of the better principles in life. We learned to do without and I think you learn from that. We learned from the surroundings and meager means. We got by."

"It was a learning experience is what it was. We all stuck together," Midge said. "I wouldn't want to do it over again."

"I had a good time," Pauline insisted.

"I don't regret it," Midge said. "I wouldn't want to do it over again."

"It makes you appreciate everything," Lucille said.

"I liked the friendships and the interesting mix of people," Florence said.

"I'll never forget one nun to this day," Midge suddenly recalled, her voice shaking with anger. "I must have been around eight or nine years old. Sister Eusabia had charge of the church. There was an altar cloth and I didn't know the first thing about crocheting then. But, oh, the cloth had a hole in it and she wanted me to mend that. She insisted I mend it. I told her I couldn't do it. I didn't know how, I didn't have the vaguest idea. So she pushed my head so it hit against one of the beds. And Margaret was so mad at her."

My last question was how they felt now about all this history—did they feel like leaving it behind?

Pauline answered, "You know what, for some reason I've just kind of gone back to it again."

"I don't know how I feel about it," Midge said. "I mean, I'm interested in it now that I'm older and I can look back. I wouldn't want to go through it again but I think we've learned a lot from it."

"But it's fun to go back and see where you were," Pauline replied.

"But I don't feel that way," Lucille said. "I'm glad to be out of it." She laughed and said, "I've been trying to run away."

"You must have a really bad feeling about it," Florence said. "I was too young to even realize it was something I wasn't supposed to be doing."

"I guess I was afraid I wouldn't get back," my mother said quietly.

14 *Cowboys & Indians*

Three miles north of Burke, South Dakota, on a dusty gravel road that wound its way through miles of fields covered with stiff, brown grass, Jack Broome stopped and pointed out his window.

"There, see that creek running through the hills?" he asked. "That land belonged to your great-granddaddy, Oliver Dion."

Jack Broome, Burke's high school principal and local historian, was giving me an impromptu tour of the area in a pickup truck with a shotgun mounted in a rack behind our heads. Five years after the interview with my aunts, after accepting their legacy of family stories, I woke up one day and knew it was time to return to South Dakota. Now I was on a three-week expedition, visiting places that were important to the Dion family, including Burke, Rapid City, and the Santee reservation. I had appeared in Broome's office that morning asking questions about my grandfather, Paul Dion, who was born on a cattle ranch near Burke; three of his daughters were also born there. This area was the jumping-off point to their years as itinerant farm laborers during the Depression.

My brothers Dick and Dave had come here a year earlier, returning home with suggestions of places to visit and people to meet, like Jack Broome. Their hunger for information, for connection to South Dakota and the places that had once been part of our family's past, inspired me to plan my own trip. They were the early scouts, while I came later, laden with tape recorder and camera.

Following the direction that Jack pointed, I saw an empty field surrounded by a sagging barbed-wire fence that dipped down toward a creek bed lined with cottonwood trees. Clumps of green vegetation followed the line of water across endless acres of dry fields. Under a piercingly blue sky, the sharp-edged tip of a butte could be seen miles away on the horizon. The only traffic on this road was an occasional startled pheasant rising up from the low underbrush.

"This was Indian land back when Oliver Dion settled here," Jack said. "This whole area, Gregory County, was part of the Great Sioux reservation."

In a treaty signed in 1868, the Teton Sioux, or Lakota, surrendered all their land east of the Missouri River. In return, they kept the Great Sioux reservation because the land was considered worthless.

"Let me guess," I said. "Somebody figured out that they wanted the land after all."

Bingo! After 1868, settlers continued to push westward in search of more land. In 1889, the Great Sioux reservation was broken into six smaller reservations: Standing Rock, Cheyenne River, Crow Creek, Lower Brule, Pine Ridge, and Rosebud. After land was allotted to tribal members, including my great-grandparents, Oliver and Susan Dion, the first sale of "excess" Indian lands in 1904 changed that area to a checkerboard of Indian and white-owned land, from open range to farms divided by barbed-wire fences.

Oliver and Susan, who were both mixed bloods, chose 160 acres near Whetstone Creek, where they could find water, trees, and enough grass to graze a herd of Black Angus cattle. Paul was the fourth of ten children they managed to raise on their ranch, despite the difficult and unpredictable weather. Cyclical droughts and killing blizzards forced homesteaders out of the state in droves, even though they had to leave behind everything they had built. Those who stayed clung to the land with a single-minded tenacity, building a community of fiercely stubborn, outspoken men and women who regarded the law as made for someone else and who treated their neighbors as part of their own family.

"I wouldn't live anywhere else," Jack said, waving his hand toward the immense empty land that surrounded us. "There's no crime to speak of. We don't lock anything around here." As we flew down unmarked roads where speed was limited only by the washboard-like surface that shook my bones, I could see a herd of cattle grazing on sparsely covered hills that rolled endlessly toward the horizon. At sunset these hills deepened to lavender, turning pink in the morning as the sun rose and meadowlarks began to warble in the fields. A few more days in this area and the Minnesota landscape would begin to seem almost claustrophobic to me. If only I could develop a tolerance for droughts, grasshopper infestations, and dust storms.

There were other, more disturbing undercurrents beneath the austere beauty of the land. South Dakota had a reputation as a state where hostility between Lakota and whites remained high for many of the same reasons that had inspired violence in Minnesota.

I asked Jack, "How well do whites and Indians get along in this area?"

"There's no problem," Jack assured me, unwilling to open sensitive issues with a stranger. "People get along just fine."

Over the next two hours, Jack gave me a whirlwind tour of the area, driving by the land once owned by Paul and Maude Dion, where Margaret, Agnes, and Florence had been born. I dutifully snapped pictures of hills covered with stubby grasses and occasional clumps of trees that served as windbreaks. Some of the fields had been planted with sunflowers, their heavy heads all facing toward the sun. Jack rattled off dates and names and bits of random information as fast as he drove, stopping once at his office to give me a handful of slides of the area. Holding one up to the light, he asked if I had heard of the black blizzards in the 1930s.

"A drought baked the land so dry that the topsoil just lifted right up," he explained. "And then the winds came, blowing the dust around so you couldn't see the road. Tractors, and even cattle, were buried."

Just before dropping me back at my car, Jack stopped at the senior citizens' center, where I met Jenny Mullen Moyer, who agreed to talk to me later about Paul Dion. Jack also suggested that I talk to Buck Mullen, a local man who had lived in the area all his life and was distantly related to my family. "Be persistent," he urged, implying that Buck might be hard to track down.

"If you need anything or you have any trouble, you just call me," Jack said, leaning out the window of his pickup. "And if I'm not home, you tell my wife and she'll get our neighbor to come and help you."

Two days later, I was standing on Jenny Moyer's doorstep, hoping to talk to her about my grandfather. I knocked and the door opened a crack. I could see a single eye peering back at me.

"I'm Paul Dion's granddaughter," I explained. "I've come to talk about the family."

"I really can't help you," Jenny said. "I don't know much about all that." The door opened wider now that she knew I carried blood belonging to a local family, especially one she was related to. Would she mind looking at some old photographs I was trying to identify? A slight hesitation, and the door swung open as she invited me in.

She fluttered a hand toward an immaculate living room and softly apologized for the mess as she led me to a small table in the dining room. She glanced at the photos I lay on the table and said she did not recognize any of them.

"When I said I remembered Paul Dion, that's all I meant, I remember him. My brother would know all about this."

Was her brother Buck Mullen?

"Yes, that's him. He would know better about all this."

I had been trying to reach Buck but failed to get past his wife's protective defenses. Jenny offered to call and see if Buck was in town playing cards, saying, "He comes in most days." She carefully dialed a number on her rotary phone with her left hand, turning slightly away from me so that I would not see her right arm hanging limply at her side.

"Hello, Helen, is that you?" she asked. "Helen, is Buck playing cards this morning? No, I'm fine. Tell him I'm sending someone down to see him." At the door she warned me about his personality. "He's a bit hard to get along with," she said, "but don't pay him any mind." She shook my hand with a delicate pressure and said goodbye, ten minutes into an interview I had expected to last most of the morning.

Two days after my ride through the back roads of Gregory County with Jack Broome, I was still on the trail of the elusive Buck Mullen. As I walked down the steps of Jenny Moyer's house toward my car, I thought how this often-fruitless hunt for information was a lot like prospecting for gold: you had to sift through a lot of ore to find something with a little sparkle to it.

The town of Burke, which is about three blocks long, has changed little in the sixty-five years since my mother's family moved away in search of more stable work than the cattle industry could provide. The windmill had been replaced with a modern water tower, and Oliver Dion's roller rink—where Paul Dion fell in love with Maude LaCroix—has been torn down. I parked in front of the bowling alley where Buck Mullen and his friends were playing cards.

The bowling alley was dark and quiet when I walked in. The empty lanes filled the back of the room and there were half-a-dozen square tables to my right. This was the bastion of retired or modestly employed men, where a game of "pitch" could be found most mornings. Only one table was being used and the six men gathered around it did not look up when I walked in, even though I was clearly a female and a stranger. They were old enough to be grandfathers and most of them looked like retired farmers in their blue jeans and baseball caps. I walked up to the group and stood politely for a moment, waiting to be noticed. Finally, realizing that no one intended to stop the game, I said, "Excuse me, is one of you Buck Mullen?"

Five heads turned slightly toward one of their members, betraying him, and the most voluble of the group nodded his head and said, "That's him right there." I moved a step closer to Buck's side of the table, where he held a hand of cards and avoided making eye contact. Buck was the only man wearing a cowboy hat, plaid shirt, and cowboy boots. His skin was dark, his eyes almost hidden by the heavy lids that now drooped at the corners. He was wiry in build, probably still wearing the same size jeans he wore forty years ago. I explained that I was the great-granddaughter of Oliver and Susan Dion, a family he was related to by marriage, a well-known name in the area a half century earlier. He was old enough to remember my grandfather Paul, and I thought he probably had known Oliver and Susan as well.

"Would you mind looking at a few photographs?"

At this, he raised his eyes to the level of my chin for a split second before turning back to his cards and mumbling, "I don't know anything about that."

I was clearly dismissed.

I could see a few barely repressed smiles beginning to form on the faces of the rest of the group as they diligently focused their attention on their cards. Buck was obviously living up to his reputation, and they were simply enjoying the sport I provided. I stood for a moment in silence while Buck continued to play, deliberately ignoring my presence. I was, however, the great-granddaughter of Oliver Dion, a rancher and patriarch who "never let any man run over him," a high compliment according to the pioneer ethic that had formed this town.

I turned away from Buck and pulled out a chair at the next table and sat down. I took out my photographs, set them on the corner of the table, and then I turned to face the group. I could see a ripple of silent amusement in their shoulders as they concentrated on the game, except for Buck, who was still turned away from me. The hand ended and Buck scooped a pile of cards toward him. The earlier spokesman said, "If you talk to her, she'll probably buy you a cup of coffee." They all laughed except Buck, who said in a low growl, "I drink too much coffee."

Another lengthy silence followed and more cards were dealt. Buck was also clearly of a type not to let anyone run over him. Finally, at the end of this hand, Buck turned his head a half-inch in my direction and said, "You're Paul Dion's granddaughter?"

Yes. More minutes and more cards passed by. I stood up, leaving my bag and the stack of photos on the table, walked up to the counter, and bought a pot of coffee and two cups. By the time I returned to the table, Buck was sitting there.

I poured us both a cup of coffee.

"I don't think I can help much," Buck said, punching out his words in a short, slow burst. "I'm eighty-three." He took a sip from his cup as if that were all that needed to be said.

I pulled the top photograph from the stack and asked if he knew the tall man with the thin dark mustache and a cowboy hat on his head who was looking at the camera with solemn attention.

"That's Oliver," he said, pointing a wrinkled finger at the photo. "He was a good man on a horse."

I explained that I had been in the area for a few days, talking to people about the Dion family. From the stories I had heard from Jack Broome and another distant relative, Mary Dion, it seemed to me that the Dions were hard-drinking, strict Catholics who may or may not have rustled cattle.

Buck thought about this for a moment, staring down into his cup, before he shook his head and said, "I never knew Oliver to rustle cattle." He looked me straight in the eye and stated, "I can't say anything against Oliver Dion," which was Buck's way of saying that Oliver was a decent, honest man. Buck had grown up in a time when extreme hardship dictated its own laws, so that a person's character was tested and judged accordingly.

From conversations with people who had known the family, I now had a rough portrait: Oliver Dion was not known to be a cattle rustler. He and Susan offered a meal to any traveler who stopped at their ranch. The family willingly lent a hand to anyone who asked, and a Dion man would always buy a round, even if it meant spending his last nickel. I mentioned these stories to Buck, and he nodded his head once in agreement. In Buck's view of the world, these were the qualities that mattered. Even by the rough rules of the early 1900s, Oliver Dion had been a man of strong character formed by the frontier and well suited to Burke.

Oliver was born in the early 1860s on Lone Tree Ranch near the Platte River. His French-Canadian father, John Dion, one of the first whites to settle in Dakota Territory, had married a full-blood Lakota woman from Rosebud. In the early 1880s, Oliver "punched cows" in Nebraska and herded cattle for the government. Oliver married Susan Langdeau in 1884, a mixed-blood woman from Rosebud. According to family myth, Susan kept a pearl-handled pistol tucked in her apron to deal with outlaws.

As an old man, Oliver reflected back on his life in an interview with the *Argus Leader* of Sioux Falls. Oliver had been at Beaver Creek after the Battle of Little Big Horn in 1876, when the Indians brought Custer's saddles, blankets, and clothing to the Indian agency. Oliver said, "More blame lies with the whites than with the Indians for that tragic battle. . . . The Indians, men, women and children were camped in the Big Horn valley, as were the soldiers, and each camp had sent out scouts. When the Indians returned to report, the tribe immediately packed their ponies, sending the women and children on ahead, the men remaining to meet an attack. The soldiers were on territory rightfully belonging to the Indians. After the battle the Indians gathered together all the soldiers' belongings and brought them to Beaver Creek, offering them for sale."

Little Big Horn intensified the feelings of distrust and hate that had been building between whites and Indians for decades. In 1890, nearly 300 Indians were massacred at Wounded Knee, ending Sioux resistance and establishing an uneasy truce between the impoverished reservations and the white settlers, who now dominated the land. By the time Oliver Dion was interviewed for the *Argus Leader*, he had learned not to mention his Lakota blood, his enrollment in the Rosebud tribe, the allotment land he lived on, or the mixed-blood Lakota woman he had married.

As the Dions' allotted land became surrounded by white settlers in a checkerboard that no longer resembled a reservation, it became easier to "pass" as white and more difficult to live as an Indian. Whites controlled the land, money, and power in the area; being "white" often meant the difference between getting a job and not being able to feed a family. After appearing in every Rosebud Indian census in the early 1890s, the Dion family had to make a choice about their identity when the reservation was opened to whites. By the time of the 1915 South Dakota census, most of Oliver and Susan Dion's family, including my grandfather Paul Dion, had shifted from "red" to "white." Whether you lived on a cattle ranch in South Dakota or in a suburb of Minneapolis, "passing" as white was one way to survive in a hostile, racist world. This was a new form of silence—one of omission—that promised safety for the price of becoming invisible.

I wondered if Buck Mullen knew how much our families had changed over time. Or maybe, by living in the same place all his life, he was more conscious of how much remained the same.

Before I left, I asked Buck if I could take his picture. "Oh, you don't want that," he said. But he sat quietly as I took two photos, even when his card-playing buddies called out for him to pucker up for the camera. I turned around and refocused the camera on the card game. I said, "Smile!" and they all ducked their baseball caps as if to hide. But in my photo, I can see a faint smile on each leathery, creased face as they all dutifully stare down at their cards.

Buck Mullen, Burke, S.D., 1997

15 *Chiefs & Scoundrels*

JULY 1997
Rapid City, South Dakota

The tinny beep of my travel alarm clock woke me with a shrill reminder that I needed to be on the road early. I had a long day of driving on two-lane highways to reach Rapid City, my next destination. After spending a week in Burke, I was on my way to meet the former Miss Indian America of 1949. My mother's cousin, Agnes LaCroix Mousel, had once been described in the *Denver Post* as "America's most beautiful Indian girl."

Rapid City is a bustling tourist mecca that traded its proximity to the Black Hills for streets lined with small shops hawking rocks, gems, silver jewelry, and *gen-u-wine* Indian artifacts. I drove as slowly as I could, looking at everything, ignoring the pickup trucks that roared past me down narrow streets that were never intended to carry heavy traffic. Every fast-food joint imaginable has a presence in Rapid City against a backdrop of pine-covered mountains and breathtaking cliffs.

Before I met Agnes, I knew only that my mother's family had lived near her in the 1930s. My mother had once talked briefly about Rapid City, leaning toward me as if to tell me a secret. She said, almost whispering, "We were white trash." And then she laughed, enjoying the surprised look on my face.

Agnes was wearing a T-shirt and jeans, her face still glowing from the exertion of mowing the lawn at Birthright, a local organization that helps unwed mothers, where she had volunteered for twenty-five years. She wore no makeup and, at seventy, she was a beautiful woman. Her face, with its high cheekbones and high-ridged nose, like my mother's, was framed by a crown of silver hair. A serious bowler sidelined by carpal tunnel in her right wrist, Agnes wore a brace on her left wrist for tendonitis. She mentioned it only when I asked, and then briefly, without complaint.

Agnes led me to her dining room, where she had spread a wealth of photos, letters, old

Agnes LaCroix Mousel, 1997

prayer books, and newspaper clippings. I looked first at the *Denver Post* photo of Agnes wearing a fifty-year-old buckskin dress covered with thousands of beads. The caption described a "raven-haired" Agnes LaCroix, twenty-one, who wore the dress to demonstrate "what the well-dressed woman wears before the inter-tribal council or in the dress circle of the Metropolitan Opera House." We had a good laugh about that.

Agnes handed me a photograph of her father, Oliver LaCroix, Jr., or Uncle Smoky, a handsome man with short black hair combed straight back, wearing a suit and wire-rim glasses. His nickname, "Smoky," was inspired by his legendary fastball during his days as a baseball pitcher at the Santee Normal Training School. He married Mary Hinman, the mixed-blood daughter of the Episcopal minister Samuel Hinman, and found work during the Depression at the Sioux Sanitarium, where Indians were treated for tuberculosis. At heart, Oliver was a musician who taught himself to play the fiddle by ear and performed at Saturday night barn dances. As the story goes, a stranger stopped at his father's home one day, needing a pair of horses to continue his long journey. Oliver, Sr., who struggled to keep his family in food and clothing, traded a pair of horses for the fiddle that became his prized possession before he passed it on to his son. Agnes still had it in her attic.

Mary Hinman's mother, Mary Myrick Hinman, had married Samuel Hinman when she was twenty-four and he was much

Oliver LaCroix, Jr., born 1888

older. They had one child, Agnes's mother, before Samuel died in 1891 at Birch Coulee in Minnesota, where he had returned to continue his work ministering to Dakota Indians. After Samuel died, his wife and daughter moved back to Santee, where Mary met and married Oliver LaCroix, Jr.

The next photographs that Agnes handed to me included a portrait of one of the most infamous characters in Minnesota's history. Mary Myrick Hinman was the daughter of Andrew Myrick, the trader who was found shot in 1862, his mouth stuffed full of grass. In the portrait, he wore a high cravat that stood stiffly beneath his dark beard; his brown eyes were slightly bulging, his lips petulant and soft. According to family legend, he tried to escape with a bag of gold that he buried in the fields where he was later found shot. Myrick's mixed-blood wife, Nancy Wapaha, hid behind the door at his trading post with her tiny baby, Mary, in one arm and a knife in the other. The Dakota had said they would kill all the mixed bloods as well as the Indians who had married whites.

Mary Myrick, her mixed-blood mother, and her full-blood Dakota grandmother, Mary Stone, were sent to the prison camp at Fort Snelling and later to the Crow Creek reservation. Agnes's mother remembered her grandmother telling her that they had lived in a stockade at Crow Creek and had nearly starved. They were given soup that was poured into a trough made of green cottonwood lumber and that was nearly impossible to eat. Her grandmother also told her that on the hundred-mile march from Crow Creek to Santee, she laid her daughter in her cradle board by the road to rest a minute. The baby was nearly run over by somebody driving a team of oxen.

Nancy Wapaha, Winyangéwin, wife of Andrew Myrick

When they finally reached Santee, they lived in tipis until frame houses were built a few years later, many of them by my great-grandfather Oliver LaCroix, Sr. During the smallpox epidemic of 1873, the family moved out of the Agency and stayed with a cousin who was a medicine man. He built a sweat lodge, and Agnes's grandmother said the sweat baths kept them from getting sick.

Agnes talked about Andrew Myrick in a matter-of-fact tone of voice, as if he was an unremarkable part of their family story. He was neither hidden away as a secret nor reviled. His egregious words and actions stood as a warning against the dangers of greed, ego, and racism. If that reminder served to produce good work by others, then that piece of shameful history had at least been transformed to something positive.

We turned our attention instead to the file of newspaper clippings about Agnes's brother, Art LaCroix, who had served three terms as Rapid City's first Indian mayor. Art had a distinctly Indian face and a strong, charming personality. After a stint on the city council, he was elected mayor in a landslide, despite Rapid City's long history of hostility between whites and Indians. Agnes said they were celebrating his election when the phone rang. The caller asked, "Do you know our new mayor is an Indian?" Why yes, they did. Art LaCroix served for thirteen years, and many would later say that he was the best mayor Rapid City has known. The city auditorium where the annual powwow is held was named after him, as well as the golf course, LaCroix Links.

Agnes said that for a long time in Rapid City, it wasn't good to admit to being Indian, that it was easier not to call attention to yourself. "I was walking home from school one day," she said, "and a neighbor boy was behind me. He called out, 'Hey, little black Sambo, where you going.' Those remarks stay with you your whole life."

Even women she had known as friends could surprise her with their unthinking remarks. One of the women in her bridge club had said, "What do you expect from an Indian?" And Agnes, whose eyes were flashing with anger as she retold the story, replied, "Wait a minute, girls, who do you think you're talking about?" And they looked at her in surprise. One of them said, "But, Agnes, you don't act Indian." The look in Agnes's eye deepened into something fierce as she recalled saying, "And just how do they act?"

I recognized her flash of fire as the same heat that came into my mother's eyes when she felt disrespected or insulted because she was Indian. Agnes and my mother shared the same gentle regard for the people around them. They listened closely, offered their opinions and stories without shyness, but just as often preferred to keep their thoughts, and certainly their feelings, to themselves. Sometimes an unthinking person misread their quiet personalities as timid. Make the mistake of trespassing on their toes, however, and something older than stone and much harder opens up in their dark eyes.

I asked Agnes if she knew how to make any of the traditional Indian foods. She said yes, she knew how to make fry bread and *wojapi*, a thick fruit sauce made from cherries. My mother had told me that when they got home from school, Maude used to make them fry bread, which they ate with maple syrup. After the interview with my aunts, she had begun to share small details from her life and to take an interest in the information I was gathering.

Agnes and the other women in my family could recall hard, painful details about the past without bitterness. They never complained about their parents, saying only that they did the best they could. They set a fine example: work hard, complain little, laugh as often as you can. Cry only when you bury a parent or a child. No matter what happens, make the best of it. And always, always, place the family first.

After leaving Agnes, I spent the blistering hot afternoon in the cool interior of the Journey Museum, an impressive new facility dedicated to preserving Indian and pioneer history that had recently replaced the old Sioux Museum. I was hoping to find a painting by Moses Stranger Horse, a Lakota artist from the Rosebud reservation.

My aunt Darlene had shown me a cedar box full of letters that Maude wrote to her daughter, Agnes, while she was away at St. Francis. In a letter dated 1933, she wrote that Moses Stranger Horse had visited them in Rapid City and given her two of his paintings. Moses Stranger Horse was born on the Rosebud reservation in 1890 and eventually became fairly well known for his landscape paintings. Unfortunately, after he died in 1941, his work became difficult to find.

After pursuing a number of dead ends, I found a library reference that said one of his paintings was owned by the Journey Museum in Rapid City. I asked a museum staff person about his work. Yes, they owned a painting by Moses Stranger Horse, and no, I couldn't see it because it was in "permanent storage." She gave me a catalog from an exhibition of contemporary Sioux painting that included his work. She also suggested that a tour of the new museum would be time well spent.

For an hour, I wandered through the exhibits, studying artifacts and learning more about the volatile and troubled history between white settlers and Lakota. The Black Hills, or Paha Sapa, are sacred land to the Lakota. The area forms the spiritual center of their world, where they pray to Wakan Tanka, the Great Spirit, and seek visions. Before the discovery of gold, the land was considered worthless by the government and ceded permanently to the Indians in the 1868 Fort Laramie Treaty.

In 1874, however, when General Custer was sent to the Black Hills to find a location suitable for a fort in order to keep trespassers out of Lakota territory, he became determined to establish the truth about rumors of gold in the hills. He sent back a note reporting there was "gold in the roots of the grass." Newspapers trumpeted the discovery, and the gold rush was on. A swarm of illegal prospectors entered the Black Hills by following a trail the Lakota called the "Thieves' Road."

That same year, prospector John Gordon attempted to elude the military and lead a wagon train into the Black Hills by following the Niobrara River. When they had safely bypassed the soldiers, they set up a log fort that was known as Gordon's Stockade.

The *Argus Leader* article I had read about my great-grandfather Oliver Dion mentioned that Oliver was one of the young men in their party. The entire group was arrested and forced to walk back to Fort Randall, where they were jailed for one month.

After the discovery of gold, the government insisted on renegotiating with the Dakota in order to purchase the Black Hills. A Black Hills Treaty Commission, with Agnes's grandfather Samuel Hinman acting as the interpreter, was charged with developing a new agreement with the Sioux. Meeting little success through negotiating, the government eventually claimed the Black Hills when Congress passed a "sell or starve" bill that forced the Lakota to sign the new treaty.

At this point, I was tired of hearing about the notoriety of some of our relatives. We certainly had our share of scoundrels whose reputations were offset only by the quiet, unremarked courage of those who simply survived war and poverty. One of the reasons stories are lost over time is that they become entangled in shame and embarrassment, as if we can change who we are by simply forgetting who we were. It would be far easier not to mention the failings of my relatives, to pretend that this story has only one side, that of heroes and chiefs.

But what if knowing the truth about the past would change the way we live in the present? What would it mean, for example, if we were held accountable not only for our own actions but also for those of history—for the actions and consequences of our relatives? Mixed bloods have sometimes been accused of taking advantage of both sides—white and Indian—neglecting their community while benefiting from the government's handouts. This is a complex issue, a tangle of hard choices, cultural values, and the need to survive. I have carried a vague feeling of shame all my life, a feeling whose origin I can't pinpoint. My mother's denial of her identity was part of it, but there was something else that lay just beyond my comprehension, as if glimpsed from the corner of my eye.

I continued to walk through the museum, arriving at a wall of photographs in the middle of the exhibit that was titled "Destruction of *Tiyospaye*," a reference that I was not familiar with. I read the short essay that explained how the extended family system, or tiyospaye, was intrinsic to Dakota culture before contact with European Americans. A good Dakota needed to be a good relative, obeying a complex system of kinship rules that governed relationships within families and community and formed an essential part of the cultural values that contributed to a peaceful community. Understanding how people were related was an important aspect of tiyospaye and one of the reasons why Indian families continue to be so aware of their ancestry. Among the government's efforts that contributed to the breakdown of tiyospaye was the introduction of the boarding school system, separating children from parents while reinforcing white cultural values.

Almost immediately, I saw a picture of a girls' basketball team that was taken in 1940 at the Holy Rosary Mission School. The girls were in their early teens, all of them wearing the same unattractive baggy bloomers and shirts, posed in a long line for the camera. Knowing that my mother was at the school at that time, I looked closer. In the middle of the row was a pair of skinny legs that could only have belonged to my mother, also known as "Sticks." She was smiling her wide, beautiful smile for the camera, unaware as yet how much her life was about to change.

I stood riveted in shock, my mother's face beaming at me from an exhibit about the destruction of tiyospaye. The present had finally caught up with the past. The two pieces cut from different puzzles—my mother's years at Holy Rosary and her life raising five children in a white suburb—came together on this wall in the Journey Museum. While I had thought only about her individual life, I saw now that she was part of something much larger than a single family's history. Her photograph was a visual metaphor for the destructive confrontation between Dakota and European cultures. Her family's struggle to survive was as much a part of that process as it was the result of their individual decisions. The shame that I carried was my family legacy, our tacit acceptance beginning generations earlier when we had been shamed for simply being Dakota.

When I returned to my motel room, I called my mother. "You're famous," I said, and told her about finding her photograph in the museum. She laughed, greatly amused by my story. I explained about the theme, destruction of tiyospaye, and she listened—but she said nothing.

Later that evening, I also called Jim Denomie, an Ojibwe from Lac Courte Oreilles reservation in Wisconsin, whom I had dated for about two years. As I told him everything I had learned that day, I could hear the deep inhale of his breath as he smoked a cigarette and listened. His quiet attentiveness was familiar, comforting, and he said little when I finished talking. Unlike the voluble advice from my dad on succeeding in business—*even if the job is mopping the floor, do the best you can*—the silence offered by my mother and Jim felt like trust that I would learn what I needed to know in my own way. There was no judgment, no encouragement, nothing to influence my own intent.

Shortly before I had started this trip, Jim had invited me to hear an Ojibwe elder speak at a small gathering of his friends. She talked about the need to remember the past, especially as it applied to Indian history. She said, "It's important to know as much as we can about ourselves." Her words seemed deceptively simple on the surface, but I kept coming back to a single question: *Why do we need to know about ourselves, our ancestors, our history? What does it matter if I know what happened to the Indian in my family, when growing up in a suburb offered safety and the comfort of a full belly?* This was my cry to the past, to the wall of photographs in the Journey Museum, to my mother's silence: *Why?*

16 *Indian Givers & Land Allotment*

JULY 1997
Santee Reservation, Nebraska

My last stop was the Santee reservation in Nebraska, where my grandmother Maude was born. I had been dreading this part of the trip. I had driven through the town of Santee once before, looked around at the tiny casino, the community center, the tribal office, the rows of plain Indian housing, and decided I was unwelcome: too white, too female, too alone. In the few minutes it took to drive from one end of town to the other, I made up my mind to leave.

This time I was more determined to find the information I needed. I crossed the South Dakota border into Nebraska and drove another thirty miles into the heart of the Santee reservation. The town of Santee, population 390, sits at the northern end of the reservation next to the Missouri River. According to my aunts, there was a piece of reservation land—160 acres that had originally been allotted to my great-grandfather Oliver LaCroix, Sr.—that still remained in the family. No one could remember how to find it. I also suspected that Oliver LaCroix was buried somewhere on the Santee reservation.

Again I drove from one end of town to the other, uncertain where I should go, and considered simply going home—I was tired, I could come back later. After all, there was no guarantee that I would even find any information. It was possible that the LaCroixs had no contact with the town of Santee or had been gone so long that the name had been forgotten. But the LaCroix land did not appear in the state's land records, nor did Oliver appear in Nebraska's death records. It was this peculiar absence of information, combined with the irresistible lure of finding reservation land still belonging to the family, that pulled me toward Santee.

I had to admit to more than the usual reluctance to introduce myself to strangers. I was afraid I would be unwelcome or judged as just another "wanna-be" looking for her Indian princess roots. Or worse, that I had come seeking proof of enough blood to allow me to enroll, thereby laying claim to the mythical wealth provided by reservation casinos. This was my fear of feeling like a minority, of experiencing the sense of "other," a feeling that human beings generally try to avoid. I was afraid of the unknown, afraid not so much of the people but of exposing myself to rejection from my family's past. Even though Oliver LaCroix had been an enrolled member, had married and raised his family on allotment land, and my grandmother Maude had been born on the reservation, I still felt I had no right to be here.

But I had an uneasy sense that to leave again would mean backing away from something in this process that was very important. To not pursue research because of these weak-kneed excuses was a form of cowardice, and ultimately my own character would pay for it. Suddenly this moment had become a turning point, a test of my desire to reconnect not only with my family's past but with a culture I had been circling from the safe distance of my research. Pushing beyond the barriers of my suburban upbringing was a first step in taking responsibility for my corner of the family's history and identity. Even if I found nothing here, at least I would have that: the information that our family had vanished from this place. I would not leave here until I had made every effort to find the land that was our most tangible link to the past.

I parked in front of the tribal office and walked in through a large, open lobby that held several chairs and a couch, most of which were filled with Indian men sitting and talking. They barely glanced up as I walked past. The woman at the desk told me I needed to see Willard Mackey, the tribal enrollment officer, and he was out with the other men. She led me back to the lobby, where Willard immediately rose to his feet, although moving slowly, as if his old bones did not respond as quickly to his mind's orders as they used to. His blue jeans hung loosely on his lanky frame, but his handshake was firm as I introduced myself. When I asked if he could help with some family history questions, he said, "Nope, can't do it." He chuckled so that I would know this was a well-played joke. "I only answer questions on Monday."

We sat in his cramped office surrounded by filing cabinets and stacks of manila envelopes. "We just moved," he explained, gesturing at the still unopened boxes behind his chair. I told him the LaCroix name and he nodded. "Yes, of course, I know the LaCroixs. Give me a minute here while I look them up."

I had seen computers on some of the other desks, but Willard pulled open a drawer in one of his cabinets and looked through paper files. As he thumbed through them, peering from under the brim of a baseball cap beaded with the insignia of the Santee tribe, Willard said he was almost retired but needed something to do with his days. "Here it is, here it is," he muttered, pulling out a number of genealogy sheets written as family trees.

Back in 1887, when the Dawes Allotment Act chopped reservations into 160-acre fragments for its members, hoping to expedite the process of "civilizing" the Indians, it also created a new system for defining who was an Indian. Traditionally, tribes did not use blood quantum, or percentage, as a way of identifying who belonged. Criteria like clan membership, namesake ceremony, intermarriage, and birth in the community were sufficient. Even the terms *mixed blood* and *full blood* originally referred to cultural characteristics rather than to racial identifiers. With the advent of the Dawes Act, Indians had to prove a certain percentage of Indian blood in order to qualify for benefits. Many tribes now use one-fourth as the criterion for tribal membership.

"Here they are," he said, pointing a knobby forefinger at a name on the page. We looked at family trees tracing back four or five generations with the percentage of blood written alongside each name in mind-numbingly precise percentages. Odd fractions like "13/32" appeared, along with the more familiar "1/4" or "1/8." Santee, or Dakota, blood was tracked separately from Lakota or other tribal blood, although sometimes they were considered together, depending on whether the question was specific to a reservation. My mother was one quarter, my grandparents Paul and Maude were both one quarter, grandmother Jenny was one half, Rosalie Marpiya Mase was full blood. My siblings and I are one eighth, the first generation to drop below the quantum needed to enroll in a tribe. As a family, we have members enrolled at Rosebud, Santee, and Sisseton, and we are lineal descendents of the Mdewakanton tribe. Blood quantum may be the easiest way to define the question of "who is an Indian," but it does not guarantee that the language and traditions—the foundation of any culture—are maintained.

Willard made copies of everything for me and then sat down behind his desk, watching as I tucked the papers in my file.

"I knew Clarence LaCroix"—Maude's younger brother—"when he lived up at the nursing home," he said. "For a while he had no money 'cause they were cashing his checks to pay his account." He leaned forward as he talked, resting the elbows of his plaid shirt on his desk. His eyes were bright with interest and curiosity, as if the enrollment business had been slow lately. He also told me that Jesse James had a son who lived in the area, Joseph Chase.

"One day Clarence told me that Jesse James and his gang were burying some of their stolen loot. There happened to be a LaCroix or two in the woods who saw them, dug up the money, moved to Minnesota and bought farm land." Willard smiled at me and shrugged his shoulders as if to say, Who can know what's true?

After replacing his file in the drawer, Willard turned to me and asked, "Would you like to see the LaCroix land?" My mouth opened slightly in surprise, leaving me with a blank, unintelligent look as I peered at him over my reading glasses.

Willard waited politely for me to catch up to his words, and I merely nodded my head dumbly. Yes, as a matter of fact, I would like to see the land. I am, after all, formed in some small way by this land, by the trails my grandmother followed through the woods, by the sage-scented air she breathed, the wild turkey she ate, the long grass that brushed her ankles in the fields. LaCroix was my grandmother Maude's maiden name, her female identity, the invisible name behind the marriage that would follow. My mother's mother, my daughter's great-grandmother, a woman born on the Nebraska prairie. Yes, I would like to see the land.

Willard climbed into my car and we drove through the back roads about fourteen miles, turning onto a dirt road that was little more than two tire tracks worn into hard-baked soil. A strip of tall weeds growing down the middle rattled the oil pan as we drove past. A barbed-wire fence separated the road from the sharply inclined fields on either side, empty except for the occasional tufts of tall prairie grass. Many of the fence posts had been topped with old cowboy boots, their pointed toes curling toward the ground. Dozens of scuffed heels saluted our passage as they preceded us down this isolated road.

After a half hour of slow, bumpy driving at five miles an hour, I said, "Willard, I think we're lost." He said nothing, turning his head to look across the rolling Nebraska hills that surrounded us.

From the corner of my eye, I could see Willard's baseball cap give a short nod. "Yup," he agreed, "we're lost." He turned back toward me and asked, "So what do you think of your trip now?" I laughed, veering around an eight-inch rut aimed at my tire.

After several more slow miles the road flattened out enough so we could turn around and pick a careful path back to the main dirt road. We found the right turn-off to the LaCroix land, following it toward the old homestead site until we found it blocked by a barbed-wire gate, which was enough to stop me from going further.

"It won't matter," Willard assured me as he climbed out and unlatched the gate, laying it to one side of the road. We drove another quarter of a mile, seeing nothing but a run-down trailer and a rusted-out car. He pointed to the trailer and said, "That's probably the original homestead; people often build on top of the old foundation."

There I was, standing at last on the dirt road that ran alongside the old LaCroix homestead. In terms of family research, there are only a few places where we seem to literally touch the past: land, homes, and graves. I could see the view that would have faced my great-grandfather's window and the field where the horses grazed after a long ride in to the Agency. I studied the land around the trailer; I would have placed my garden there, in the full sunlight. No doubt the road was nearly impassable during winter blizzards and summer flash floods. But there was a simple, plain beauty to it: low hills, a thick grove of bur oak, willow, and cottonwoods that grew along a nearly dry creek. The land was considered to be a poor choice for farming and of marginal value as pasture.

But to Oliver LaCroix, it would have meant enough land to settle down and raise a family. He was among the first generation to receive allotment land in 1885, a parcel of 160 acres on the reservation. The portion still owned by the family is now leased to the Santee tribe. Jenny Felix LaCroix also received an eighty-acre allotment, which she sold after Oliver's death. The small annual checks—two or three dollars—that my mother and her sisters still receive is their share of the lease payment for Oliver's land.

Virginia Felix, known as Jenny, met Oliver shortly after they both moved to the Santee reservation in the early 1880s. Jenny came from Mendota with her parents, Peter or Pierre Felix, a mixed blood who spoke both French and Dakota, and Marguerite Bellecourt, Ge-Shah-Day-Quay, an Ojibwe woman from Mille Lacs. Jenny's grandmother, Rosalie Frenier, Mazas Nawin, or Iron Lady, stayed behind in Mendota. Her father, François Frenier, was a mixed-blood fur trader who married a Sisseton woman, Wiyantóicewin. François had a twin brother, Narcisse—Cepka, or Twin—and another brother, Louison, who traveled with the explorer Joseph Nicollet. Her great-great-grandfather was Charles Jacques Frenier, who was married to the daughter of Tokokotipixni, He Who Fears Nothing, a powerful Yankton chief.

Only one of Oliver and Jenny's eleven children, Roy, died as an infant, leaving behind a large brood of siblings close in age:

Oliver, Jeanette, Henry, Maude, Raymond, Agnes, Mae, Clarence, Lillian, and Marie. The children grew up speaking French and English, although Jenny had also learned the Dakota language as a child. Years of wildly erratic weather meant that survival was harsh and unpredictable; droughts and locusts seemed intent on punishing anyone who dared live in such an inhospitable area. My grandmother Maude was born in 1893, into a cycle of droughts that forced white farmers to abandon their farms, leaving the Indians in a "miserable, starving condition," according to the Indian agent at that time, Joseph Clements. Fortunately for the LaCroix family, chokecherry and wild plum trees grew near their creek, offering a steady supply of fruit for canning and making jams and jellies, while pheasants, wild turkeys, and white-tailed deer provided wild game for the table.

Jenny Felix LaCroix, at left, and six of her children, early 1910s: Agnes (standing), Lillian (with doll), Maude, Clarence, Oliver, Mae

Pauline had showed me a photograph of the original farmhouse, not much bigger than the present trailer, with a small, shed-like room attached to the side, where Jenny had given birth to her babies. Pans of boiling water heated on the wood stove inside the house would have been carried outside to the separate entrance into the small room. One of the LaCroix babies was delivered in the shed in midwinter when the temperature dropped so low that a cloud of steam rose as the baby's torso pushed its way toward the night air.

When my aunt took that picture in 1975, the windows were half-boarded shut, as if the house had long since been abandoned. This was the home that Oliver had built in the late 1800s, just as he had used his carpenter skills to build many of the original homes and buildings on the reservation. In the photo, three of Oliver's children, Clarence, Agnes, and Lillian, were peering into the lean-to that had been built on the back of the house. Their older sister, my grandmother Maude, had died thirteen years earlier.

As I snapped pictures of the land where Maude grew up, I could see her running across the fields, picking berries in the summertime. Did she walk to school, carrying her lunch in a pail, holding her younger brother by the hand? One weekend my sister and I stayed with her at her cabin on Medicine Lake. I thought she was somber and somewhat intimidating, but also gentle, accepting us as we were, two gawky, shy girls around seven and eight years old.

One evening when we were sitting on her back step watching the sky slowly darken enough to see the stars, Maude suddenly grabbed hold of the railing and stood up, moving with unaccustomed haste. She hurried through the back door into the kitchen, where we could hear the rattle and clank of pots and pans. She reappeared carrying two large glass Mason jars and moved down the steps with the same purposeful stride that had carried her inside. Maude set off across the yard toward the lake, where the weeds and cattails grew near the water. We hurried right behind her, almost tripping on her heels. As she grew closer to the weeds,

she stopped suddenly and pointed without saying a word. I looked, my sister looked, and there, beyond the end of her wrinkled finger, was a handful of glittering diamonds tossed into the dark bush. I held my breath in wonder as dozens of fireflies winked and glowed.

Maude crept forward more slowly and then stood near the weeds for a moment, allowing the fireflies to adjust to her presence so they would not fear her. Suddenly, she leaped into the air, her thick-soled shoes a full inch from the ground, as her arms shot out and captured a firefly, holding it ever so gently in her cupped palms. She carried this treasure back to us, my sister and I frozen in awe, and motioned at the jar on the ground. I held it up to her and she carefully released this first firefly into it. I slid the lid on quickly and then beheld the miracle of my tiny prisoner, still glowing and sparkling in captivity. Maude had already returned to the bush. She stood poised for another graceful, age-defying leap that would forever transform her in my eyes from a somber woman to this mystical being who flew toward the heavens.

When there were two or three fireflies in each jar, Maude turned back toward the house. As she emerged in the light from the back porch, she became once again the careworn grandmother I had known, a woman who darned socks with fingers grown hard and calloused from years of rough work. But that night I had seen those same fingers work their magic, cupping a spark of light with infinite gentleness, her silence an eloquent reminder of how needless words can be. The first time I saw my mother cry was at Maude's funeral in 1962.

But here, on her father's land near the creek, Maude had been a young girl who had hoped to become a nurse until her father's sudden death called her home from school to help her mother. She returned to a house in mourning, with nothing to break the quiet except the wind and the cry of hawks. Seven years passed before she found a way to leave again by falling in love and marrying a young cowboy she met at his father's roller rink.

The pictures I took would show none of this. Only a bare field

with nondescript trees remained; only the careful notation beneath the photograph would remind me of their importance. Visiting an old homesite tends to be anticlimactic, a moment steeped in significance and yet ordinary. Willard was patient and silent, allowing me to take my time. I bent down and ran my fingers through the dust, picking up a small pebble, which I tucked in my pocket.

I stood for a few minutes, simply listening. The day was warm and still, with few leaves moving. The silence of the LaCroix land felt like an absence: of people, of animals, of a house left standing empty. There was nothing threatening in it, nor was there invitation.

Over the rest of that afternoon and much of the next day, Willard rode with me through the back roads of the reservation. We had lunch at the combination gas station/café with bars on its windows, sitting at a long common table with people who knew Willard. Many of them said to me, "I've got a cousin/wife/ex-husband who's related to the LaCroixs." At one point during our drive, Willard waved his hand at the hills and said, "The Frasiers and Freniers and Robinettes were all interrelated. They all came to this area and intermarried until we're all 'kissing cousins.'" He smiled, acknowledging that we were most likely distant kin.

Willard also showed me the Catholic cemetery that sat high on a hill above the Missouri River, impossible to locate without a guide from the area. I had hoped to find the gravesites where family was buried, especially Oliver LaCroix, but we sat in the car after Willard warned, "I wouldn't want you to go in there and get bit by a rattler." Earlier at the office he had said that they kept the doors closed on the front side of the building so the rattlers wouldn't creep in.

"In August," Willard said, warming to his subject, "when they're losing their skin, it covers their eyes so they can't see. They pretty much strike at anything." Just as I felt my eyes grow large at the thought of these blindfolded rattlers striking wildly, I heard a soft laugh from the man who was sitting at the desk in the next office. Willard, it seemed, knew a lot of stories about rattlesnakes. Nonetheless, prowling through graveyards was postponed for another, colder season.

When I brought Willard back to the tribal office, he stopped by the front door and pointed out his name on the plaque. It read, "Willard Mackey, Tribal Chairman." Willard had already taken his turn at steering the tribe toward an uncertain future.

As I said goodbye to Willard, his earlier question—"So what do you think of your trip now?"—still hovered between us. I shook his hand, feeling like an amnesiac whose memory has begun to return a small piece at a time, as if I had woken from a long nap to find family surrounding me who were familiar and new, all at once. I was recovering the culture that lies within generations of family whose memories are so often forgotten or discarded as no longer useful. Whether they are Indian or Swedish, these are the people and the places that mold us, long before we're born. To Willard, however, I just smiled and said, "It doesn't get any better than this."

A year later, I came back to Santee with my brother Dave, still hoping to find Oliver LaCroix's grave. When we asked for Willard at the tribal office, his daughter Ellie told us that he was in the hospital with pneumonia. "Maybe Tuffy can help you," she added, referring to Willard's younger brother, Clement, who also worked at the tribal office. He was usually around in the afternoon except that no one could find him. I said we would stop back the next afternoon, our last day in town, and perhaps we would find Tuffy then. It was now mid-November and unseasonably warm, raising my old fear of rattlesnakes in the cemeteries.

On the nine-mile drive back to Highway 12, the Santee reservation felt almost familiar as we passed easily recognized landmarks: an animal skull mounted on a rancher's front gate, the breathtaking view of the Missouri River from the bluffs that surround Santee. The landscape was rugged, mile after mile of steep hills covered with wild sage and cactus. When the reservation was first established in 1869, the land was described by a visiting superintendent as "the roughest and least valuable tract of country I have seen in Nebraska, a large part of it . . . only fit for pasturage."

Marginal in value as this land might be, its austerity was part of its rough appeal. The soft light in late fall lay sepia shadows on the hills, while the bare trees stood in subtle, gray relief to the deep green of the cedars and junipers. As we drove west toward Niobrara, another tiny town just outside the western boundary of the reservation, the road dipped down to the level of the Missouri River. Thanks to a new dam, there was water on either side of this two-lane highway.

That night we stayed in a two-bedroom cabin in the middle of Niobrara State Park, over 1,200 acres of open land that straddled the confluence of the Niobrara and Missouri rivers. As the sun set on the far side of the hill, white-tailed deer strolled through the fields, seemingly undisturbed by the occasional loud boom of a hunter's gun or the poignant music my brother played on the guitar that always traveled with him. How appropriate that a musician should search for Oliver LaCroix's grave, playing for a man who loved his fiddle.

The next morning we began the task of retracing the history of Oliver LaCroix's allotment land, hoping to understand through his example the complex land policies implemented by the federal government over the past century and more. The policy of allotment that was legislated in the late 1880s—reservation land would now be owned individually, or in severalty, by tribal members—decimated the land base of many reservations, as land moved quickly into the hands of white settlers. Land policies had become one of the most significant, destructive, and duplicitous means by which the government essentially stole Indian land.

Up until the late 1800s, allotment was characterized as another means of "civilizing" the Indians by investing them with land and citizenship. Each 160-acre allotment was to be held in trust for twenty-five years, a period of time that would allegedly allow Indians to acquire farm and land-management skills. After the trust period, Indians would each receive a patent allowing them to sell their land if they chose. Unfortunately, lacking either farm skills or any experience in selling land, Indians often sold their allotments for a fraction of their worth.

The Santee were considered one of the most acculturated tribal groups, largely due to the efforts of missionaries like Samuel Hinman. Yet even their willingness to adapt to farming was compromised by the marginal quality of the land and the cycles of drought that destroyed successive years of crops. The Dakota also discovered that it was easier to lease out marginal land than to farm it, greatly extending the amount of land under the control of white settlers.

After the Santee reservation was allotted in 1885, over 42,000 acres were opened to white settlers. Unfortunately, children born to the original allottees on the reservation, like my grandmother Maude, found themselves without access to reservation land as they came of age.

The rapacious desire for Indian land continued to put pressure on legislators, shifting their philosophy of gradually moving Indian tribes toward economic independence to a belief that tribes no longer required federal protection and that Indian land belonged in the hands of whomever it would best serve. In a landmark legal decision around 1900, *Lone Wolf v. Hitchcock*, the Supreme Court ruled that tribal lands belonged to the United States, which could make whatever rules it chose. This was a final, silent defeat for control of the tribes' own land.

In 1906, Roosevelt's new Commissioner of Indian Affairs, Francis Leupp, extended this new philosophy with a rule change that would have devastating consequences. The protection provided by the trust period was eliminated and a fee-simple title was granted to allottees instead. This removed any restrictions on the sale of Indian land. Leupp's intent was simple: "The Indian who can speak English and who has been educated by the government should be free to sell his lands and to sink to the bottom."

Further allotment of Indian lands was prohibited in 1934, under the Indian Reorganization Act, and some provisions were made to rebuild tribal land bases. By that time, however, the damage had been done. Ultimately, allotment land policies had resulted in a staggering loss of land through deception and manipulation, a process that had been rationalized by narrow, racist interpretations of Indian needs.

At the land office we spoke to Bud Twiss, who said he knew Art LaCroix, my mother's cousin in Rapid City. His own wife was related to the LaCroix family. He also said that most of the LaCroix allotment land had been bought back by the tribe, while the remaining interest had been leased. Oliver died before gaining title to his land, so ownership had passed to his heirs. This had led to the equally complicated issue of heirship, and the near impossibility of getting a large group of descendents to agree to sell, which was why we still had allotment land in our family.

Of more immediate concern, however, was finding the graves of Oliver and his son Clarence. None of our extended family in Minnesota knew where they were buried. I was afraid that if we didn't learn soon, that information would be lost to the family when people like Willard, already seventy-seven, became the last, fragile holders of this knowledge.

Locating graves had become an obsession, my own private compulsion to know where family members were buried, especially the relatives whose stories and graves had been lost or forgotten. After learning as much as possible about relatives—where they were born, whom they married, the history they lived through—it felt oddly incomplete if I didn't also learn where they were buried. Their reconstituted memory floated in space, ghostlike, without that knowledge. The grave gave them roots, literally—a place where they were permanently attached.

On my previous trip I had wandered on my own through a few of the old Santee cemeteries without finding any LaCroix family. Tuffy was our last hope for finding Oliver on this trip.

We walked into the tribal office past a long, white limousine, complete with driver waiting patiently in the front seat. There doesn't seem to be a great deal of money around the Santee reservation, its tiny casino notwithstanding, so it was surprising to see this sudden wealth flashed around. We ran into Ellie as we came in, who told us that people from the Prairie Island reservation had come down to offer their advice on negotiating with the state regarding casinos. Tuffy was part of a large group of men sitting in the meeting room, but he came out immediately when Ellie touched his shoulder.

He was shorter than Willard, and softer, both in body and personality. He also wore a baseball cap with the Santee insignia beaded on the front. We shook hands and he offered to guide us to the cemetery. "Meet me out front," he said. "I'll be the one in the old Ford pickup whose paint job keeps trying to outrun the truck."

We parked out front, waiting near the limousine. Tuffy pulled up next to us in his truck, bits of rust making lace out of the body above the wheels, and rolled down his window. "I thought you two came in the limousine," he yelled, and then laughed as he pulled ahead.

As we drove toward the far end of town, Tuffy suddenly swerved into the other lane in front of an oncoming truck. As he pulled back into his own lane, the other truck swerved toward him, finishing the dance that Tuffy had begun. As they passed, both arms came out of the driver's windows and waved as they drove by.

We turned down a dirt road that led toward the boat basin, a popular fishing spot on the river. Following this narrow road another quarter mile, we turned again on an unmarked road, this one little more than two tire tracks leading through a field. I could see a large white cross sprouted above us on the hill and a small cemetery near the top. We parked behind Tuffy's truck and followed him as he checked names on gravestones.

"Here he is," he said, without fanfare, pointing to the tidy gravestone bearing Oliver LaCroix's name. The grave was remarkably well tended, considering it had weathered ninety-five years on that hill. Oliver had a magnificent view of the Missouri River, the deltas that crisscrossed the water, the patches of tall reeds that glowed almost orange in the sun, and the white stone cliffs that lined the opposite shore. Just down the hill in a more recent addition to the cemetery were the graves of two of Oliver's children, Clarence LaCroix and Agnes St. Arnaud. Thankfully, not a rattlesnake in sight.

Now, Tuffy could have turned on his heel and left at this point, his sense of obligation to us fulfilled by finding Oliver's grave. Not only was he busy helping out at the tribal college, managing the emergency systems for the reservation, and overseeing the grants for developing recreation areas along the river, he also suffered from a blood clot that sapped his strength and occasionally disturbed his short-term memory. Instead, he chose to stand in the wind with us, talking about the family and the reservation as if sensing the hunger for information that had driven us here, hundreds of miles from Minnesota.

"Clarence loved to fish," Tuffy said, repeating a statement that has been said about many LaCroixs. He also said that Clarence was a big man, "industrious and well-liked."

"After I was diagnosed with my heart condition, the aunts kept a real close eye on me," Tuffy said. "If my window shade didn't come up at the right time, there would be all kinds of soup showing up. One day Clarence came with a bowl of soup and said, 'I have to stay while you drink this.' I said, 'Clarence, I've already had four bowls of soup!'" He laughed, saying he ended up with six bowls of soup that day.

Tuffy also told us that people were slowly returning to live on the reservation, drawn by its distance from the problems of urban living and the promise of two and a half acres of land plus access to tribal health services. To be eligible, returnees had to be enrolled as members; an individual could also be "adopted" into the tribe.

The issue of enrollment is the line that has been drawn in our family between my mother and her children, a separation that raises questions of identity and heritage that are political in origin. This was, perhaps, the barrier I had felt when first approaching the Santee reservation. Our family had intermarried until the Indian blood of my generation was no longer sufficient for enrollment, so the sense of belonging in either a political or familial sense was effectively closed to us. But we were Dakota by heritage, by our interest in the past, by our presence on that November day on the Santee reservation. The kindness shown by Willard, Tuffy, and everyone else we had met welcomed us in as prodigal family but not as members of the community.

Nonetheless, I found comfort in the welcome I received there. This search could easily have ended at the front door to the tribal office without the generosity of people like Willard and Tuffy and everyone else who had acknowledged us as family. I was beginning to understand the pull of the reservation on people who return again and again, who mention it first when asked where they are from. This is the place where my family lived, where there is land that still bears our name, where every third person seems to be related somehow as distant kin. Remembering graves, names of grandparents, aunts and uncles, retelling family legends is regarded as part of the ordinary business of each day, the simple reality of tiyospaye. There was no surprise in our return to the reservation. It is, after all, what Indian families do after they move away.

It was also the first step on the road to recovering a connection to our Indian blood that was not defined politically in terms of its "quantum." This was the simple, humble pulse of blood that seeks its own, that returns to the heart because it must.

17 *Spirit Car*

1997
South Dakota

I don't tell this to a lot of people, but sometimes I drive a spirit car. Ordinarily, I drive a Toyota Corolla, a dependable vehicle that suits an earnest, straightforward writer like myself. But after three weeks of traveling around South Dakota digging up information about long-dead relatives, I need something better suited to their needs.

I don't remember when I first noticed the change. Maybe it was after the time I spent alone in the Badlands, at the end of the tourist season, when I rented a cabin before realizing that I was the only person staying that night, and the next night. Even the staff went home at the end of the day. If I wanted to call my daughter or Jim, I had to use the pay phone on the outside of the main building, a block from my cabin, dropping my quarters while I watched the shadows lengthen around me. Maybe that's when I finally realized that I was not traveling alone.

These long weeks in South Dakota had taught me that there was more to research than history books and genealogy charts. I had become a hunter, silent and still, stalking the family myths hidden in the hills. One day I realized that the wind had its own voice and the land listened to my footsteps. And my entire back-seat was filled with relatives who wondered why I wasn't paying more attention to their part of the family story. That's when it all started to come together, the mess of facts and old photographs and the smell of sun-baked fields, my own myth rising up from fragments of the past.

Of course, my relatives also like to travel in style. I would not ask my great-grandfather Oliver Dion, for example, a cattle rancher from the Old West, to ride in a Toyota. The thought of his long legs, tall hat, and big shoulders somehow squeezing down into my bucket seats is ridiculous. I have no choice but to get a spirit car, a big old Cadillac with fins, fancy hubcaps, leather seats, and power windows, something in sky blue that blends with the horizon, whipping up a gust of warm wind as we roar down the highway.

I need a big trunk, too, for some of these relatives like to travel with a lot of baggage. Take great-grandma Jenny LaCroix, for example. Always talking about the nursing home and how she's not going back there anymore. No sir, her bags are packed and stowed in the trunk. She asks if we can go fishing, peering once into her large black purse as if something is missing. I smile politely and say, "We'll see," just as I used to say to my eleven-year-old daughter.

I tell you, after a couple of weeks on the road, I'm tired of the squabbling. It's a car full of grandmothers and grandfathers, aunts and uncles, crying infants, and everyone wants a seat by the window. I tell them right up front, "I've got work to do, so come along for the ride but don't get in the way." Sooner or later they all come up to the front seat and whisper stories in my ear. I remember them as best I can, the way a person remembers a dream upon waking. They seem to know that I need help to find the way back, and so they come, pleased to be remembered. As I drive past the familiar landmarks at Santee, grandmother Maude comes and sits with me, her hands folded in her lap. Just before we leave the reservation she turns and says, "It was an act of love," and then faces back toward the window.

Of course, it's all family, so sooner or later there's trouble. The South Dakota cowboys are always poking fun at the Nebraska hayseeds, and then the shooting starts, only obviously no one gets hurt. At least it drowns out the praying and the nonstop clicking of the rosary beads by some of our Catholic relatives.

It gets real quiet again when I'm coming up on the Minnesota border. You might say that a spirit is really a restless memory and they love riding the back roads around the reservation or following the fence line for miles, checking for gaps in the wire. I've learned to recognize them the way the wind will suddenly cloak itself in a handful of dust and swirl across a cemetery. "Welcome, welcome," the spirits say, bending the branches of old, tired cedar trees. But when I come close to the border, I know they start missing home. I tell them, "That's okay, ride as far as you can." About the time I hit the bright lights on the edge of the city, I'm back in my old Toyota, with only the faint scent of wild sage in the air.

18 *Turning Point*

NOVEMBER 1999
Minneapolis, Minnesota

My mother and I sat together in the small room where she had begun hormone-based chemotherapy, both of us relaxed in La-Z-Boy recliners, facing straight ahead at the opposite wall with its generic waterfall print.

We were quiet for a moment, thinking about the scrap of letter I had just shown her from the cedar chest that preserves Maude's handwritten letters to her daughter Agnes at St. Francis. A single page had been saved from the long-awaited letter Maude wrote to Lucille in 1942, telling her they had the money to bring her home.

> I still like the Black Hills if they would only get the rain they need. We have a nice garden we appreciate that too we have the nicest radishes and onions to eat now and lettuce pretty soon. I surely do wish you were here, but it won't take long for you to get here after you get started. Fort Snelling soldiers just returned Saturday. We live just across the big bridge from the fort. The church we go to is 100 years old just think of it. But its so nice almost covered with vines. Well Lucille I hope you will be home in a week or so now. So be a nice girl and don't get too lonesome.
>
> Give our best regards to Father Zimmerman and the sisters that we know. I will close now. You ask Father if he can find out the best way for you to come by bus or train. You can come either way. Well dearie I must close with love and best wishes to you hoping to see you soon.
>
> Ever Your loving Mother

I asked my mother once how she had reacted when she found her house empty. She said, "I don't know, I think I was in shock, I don't remember anything." She went back to her narrow bed at Holy Rosary and made it through the rest of the day, and the next day, and the next. Days became months, turned into summer, when she should have been home with her family. At fourteen, after a year away from home, she waited another year until her mother's letter finally arrived.

"Holy Rosary made me tough," she said once in response to something I told her about my daughter. "Jodi is not as tough as her grandmother." I looked at her, an IV tube trailing from her thin arm, a happy smile on her face as she sipped the decaf mocha latte I had brought her. She was tough. Not hard, or mean, or bitter, or angry at anyone who had ever hurt her. Just tough.

These regular visits to the oncologist became a time for us to talk about her family. She was not a storyteller nor was she accustomed to thinking about her life in terms of what it meant. But unlike her reticence when we were growing up, she now would tell me what she remembered, and she read the stories that I wrote. Sometimes she commented and sometimes she said nothing at all. I wanted only to know that I had captured the story, or the person, in a way that felt true to her.

When she read the story about being left at Holy Rosary, she said simply, "That feels right." But when I described Maude as somber and intimidating, she said vehemently, "Oh no, she wasn't like that at all. I think she must have been sick already with cancer when you girls went to visit." Maude catching fireflies was the person she remembered.

The nurse came in periodically to check on my mother, offering candy for her blood sugar if needed, or draping a cotton blanket across her legs. My mother was so cheerful and so grateful for the nurse's small attentions that she generally spent a little extra time fussing over her, tucking the blanket around her legs so that she didn't grow cold from the inactivity.

"You don't need to sit here," my mother said to me. "I'm fine. You've got too much work to do to waste time here." There were no magazines or television in the room, but she would sit contentedly for the next two hours with nothing more than her own thoughts to entertain her.

I told her stories about my travel in South Dakota. On a trip to Holy Rosary, I had talked to a lively Jesuit priest dressed in a faded black cassock and tennis shoes, with a blond beard that appeared to be dipped in silver. When I mentioned the painter Moses Stranger Horse to him, he jumped up and said, "We have one of his paintings." He flew down the hall, calling greetings to students, finally stopping in front of a door that he unlocked with a janitor-size set of keys that hung from his belt. Inside the room, on a long, cluttered table, was a large painting covered with a thin piece of plywood. Together we removed the covering to reveal a romantic landscape of mountains painted in soft blues and purples against the backdrop of a pastel sky, with several Indians traveling around a serene lake. Two holes had been drilled into the canvas where it had once been mounted to a wall. Actually seeing the painting, however, meant far less to me than finding it. I felt as if I had somehow returned it to my grandmother Maude.

My mother was increasingly curious about the information I brought back from my trips. She listened attentively, occasionally asking questions or comparing my details to her memories. As we talked about family members, I also explained the government's policies regarding land allotment and boarding schools. She told me that some of her own prejudice toward Indians came from the man that one of her aunts had married, an abusive alcoholic with whom she had moved to the Rosebud reservation. Accepting his behavior as a stereotype, I told her gently, is a form of internalized racism. You turned against your own heritage, gnawing it off like a foot caught in a trap.

She nodded and closed her eyes, resting her head against the back of the chair. I looked at her for a long moment, seeing how her cheekbones stood out against the tired lines of her face, how her hair had thinned. As it had with her older sister, Margaret, who had died a few years earlier, the rigors of cancer and its treatment emphasized her Dakota features, even as it yellowed her skin. Now she looked more like her cousin Art LaCroix, when he spoke to our large group at a family reunion in Rapid City.

I had sat at a table with my mother, my brother Dave, my sixteen-year-old daughter Jodi, and my partner, Jim Denomie. Art had talked about the long history of the LaCroix family and how we should be proud of who we are. As I listened, I looked around the room and observed how the Indian and white blood had mingled, how some faces were dark with classic Dakota profiles, like Art LaCroix's, while others, like mine, never saw daylight without a sunscreen. Yet we were all family, all bound together by a common history. Our heritage exists because it is remembered, a responsibility that is shared by every family member.

19 'Til Death Do Us Part

MAY 2000
St. Paul, Minnesota

"Of course I know the LaCroix family," Alan said, handing me a file. "A lot of the LaCroix family history was formed right here in Minnesota. One of the LaCroixs was a Renville Ranger." He gave me a copy of his book, *Through Dakota Eyes*, a collection of first-hand accounts from Dakota people about the 1862 war.

Sometimes a conversation with the right person is all that's needed to turn in a new direction. Alan Woolworth, an anthropological historian and retired staff member at the Minnesota Historical Society, was exactly that person. He has spent much of his career helping local tribes research their history and protect significant sites such as Pilot Knob Hill in Mendota. Like Willard Mackey at Santee, Alan is an elder, a fragile provider of information to confused souls like me. When I first knocked on his door, I could see a brightly colored star quilt hanging on the opposite wall, a thank-you gift from a local tribe.

I was hoping that Alan's expertise could help me move one more generation back in time. I was searching for information about Louis LaCroix and Rosalie Marpiya Mase, Oliver LaCroix's parents, one of the furthest generations on record in that branch of the family. I was especially interested in Rosalie's life as a full-blood Dakota woman in Minnesota and her marriage to a white trader. Few records were kept during the early 1800s, and many of those had been destroyed or lost.

When I mentioned the LaCroix family, Alan nodded his head immediately.

"Louis LaCroix was a French-Canadian fur trader and one of the earliest settlers in Renville County. Your great-great-grandmother, Rosalie, was from the Mdewakanton tribe." He pointed to their names on my genealogy sheets, which were lying open on his desk.

"You know, don't you, that your relatives were involved in the Dakota War? They took refuge at Fort Ridgely when the fighting started."

Well, no, I didn't know. Up until that point, I had assumed that I should look first in South Dakota, where my mother grew up. I thought we were a family of the plains, people accustomed to drought, fierce winds, and a long, low horizon. I had followed the path my grandfather's family, the Dions, had taken as they moved across the state. Along the way, I had retraced my grandmother Maude as far as the Santee reservation, but I had yet to look beyond that short history, never questioning my assumption that the paternal line was driving the family's destiny, as it had driven mine. Nor had I considered the bigger question of how or why they came to live at Santee. There were no family stories remaining about the 1862 war, and Fort Ridgely meant nothing more to me than the campground my daughter and I had abandoned on our trip many years earlier.

When I opened the LaCroix file, however, I realized that their story had begun in Minnesota, not South Dakota, and that they had been part of the 1862 war. Long before the war began, however, traditional Indian culture was already under attack from a number of directions. The holy state of matrimony turned out to be one of the government's best weapons.

Rosalie Marpiya Mase was a Dakota woman, or a Santee Sioux, born around 1830. In a statement made for the 1856 Lake Pepin Sioux List of Claimants, her husband, Louis, testified that Rosalie was a full blood from the Wahpekute tribe and their children were half blood. He signed with his "X." The government was considering a reservation for "half-breeds" at Lake Pepin as a solution to the thorny question of whether to consider mixed bloods as

"Indians" or "whites" for purposes of annuity payments and other tribal benefits. The Lake Pepin scheme failed, but those who qualified were given scrip that could be exchanged for land. Rosalie's claim for her children was disputed, indicating that the tribe may have chosen not to recognize her after her marriage to a white man. This was one of the few written records in which the LaCroix family appears.

It was also possible that Rosalie may have been related to Iron Cloud, Wacouta's second chief, who belonged to a Mdewakanton band that settled in the village of Haminnechan, or Wood-Water-Mountain, an area that is now the town of Red Wing. Iron Cloud may have been her own name or it might have been assigned to her as her family name, along with Rosalie, at the time she was baptized Catholic. Indian names, which were given as part of an important ceremony in a Dakota person's life, were replaced with randomly chosen Christian names selected by missionaries as part of "civilizing" the tribes.

Rosalie's husband, Frederic Louis LaCroix, known as Louis, was a French Canadian from Missouri who was born in the early 1800s. He worked as a fur trader for the Hudson's Bay Company, which hired *voyageurs* to travel and manage the fur posts, trading manufactured goods—guns, knives, axes, pots and pans, blankets, cloth—for furs. Louis learned to navigate the unruly Mississippi River in a flat-bottom boat before establishing his own trading post at Louisville in Scott County and near Morton in Renville County. In general, French Canadians were considered generous and respectful of Indian beliefs, with little interest in the sedentary agricultural life of the English-speaking Protestants, who also despised French Catholicism.

On January 18, 1848, deep in the heart of Minnesota's bitter winter, a Catholic ceremony formalized the marriage between eighteen-year-old Rosalie and Louis, who was at least twenty years older. Their eldest son, Fred, had been born a month earlier. With a fragile infant to care for, it's likely that they were married at their home on LaCroix Creek near the Minnesota River, where Louis had established one of his trading posts, when Father Ravoux traveled through the area offering Catholic services. Their marriage inadvertently thrust Rosalie and Louis straight into the divisive issues that now surrounded intermarriages between whites and Indians, a situation that had little to do with personal relationships. Marriage was political, economic, pragmatic, and, in terms of the government's agenda, racist.

Given the large difference in their ages, their marriage was probably arranged to strengthen a trade alliance between LaCroix and Rosalie's tribe. It was common, even essential, for traders to marry Indian women in order to establish strong kinship ties with the tribe. An Indian wife guaranteed a certain amount of loyalty from the tribe's hunters, as well as providing the trader with an interpreter, guide, and companion.

In the early decades of the nineteenth century, when traders were few in number, intermarriages with Indian women seemed to be full of advantages for both sides. Traders were absorbed into the tribe through marriage and adoption, making them relatives with all the rights and responsibilities of kinship. The tribe's hunters would be loyal to the trader while guaranteeing for themselves a steady source of trade goods. As long as the traders remained few in number and had little impact on the tribe's affairs, intermarriages continued to flourish.

By the time Louis and Rosalie married in 1848, however, the fur trade had greatly declined, and Indians relied more heavily on the annuity payments and goods provided by the government. Traders like Louis shifted from furs to exchanging goods in anticipation of these annuity payments, extending credit until they were received.

Tribes were also beginning to realize that intermarriages had unleashed a new, and powerful, force within Indian culture: the "half-breed." Torn between two cultures, mixed-blood children grew up with varying degrees of loyalty to both sides, depending on which community they were raised in. Some identified closely with their tribe, spoke only Dakota, and became influential in tribal councils. Others adopted the lifestyle of whites, learning to farm, speak French or English, and read and write. The uncertainty over a mixed-blood person's cultural loyalty created a cultural limbo that persists to this day.

While Indians had accepted intermarriage as a mutually beneficial, reciprocal arrangement between tribes and traders, the government had other, darker motives for supporting mixed marriages. They were considered an effective means of destroying tribes by injecting "superior white blood" into inferior native bloodlines, even if the marriage was to a lower-class trader. Mixed marriages meant that in families like that of Louis and Rosalie, the children's Indian blood would be diluted, with European cultural values formed from the earliest days of childhood. It was far more difficult to introduce change to traditional families, to reach full-blood children with the values that Europeans wished to instill in them.

The goal of "civilizing" Indians was much easier within a mixed marriage in which the European husband assumed what was considered his natural role as head of the household by both gender and race. As an equal if complementary partner in marriage with a Dakota man, a Dakota woman would not have the name of her husband. Her children and all domestic property belonged to the woman and her family. Women played a vital role in Dakota spiritual beliefs and were also invited to sit on councils and become medicine women. Descent was traced through the maternal line and the honor of the family was in a woman's hands.

Marriage with a European man meant that Dakota women were now placed in a subservient role and considered the property of the husband. This was a devastating change to the status of Dakota women like Rosalie. The LaCroix children were given only Christian names and raised Catholic in a community of mixed-blood families who lived near, but outside, the reservation itself. *The History of Renville County*, published in 1916, bestowed on Rosalie's seven half-blood children the distinction of being the first white babies born in the township, with no mention at all of their Dakota blood. A century later, Lucille's five children would be the first generation not eligible for tribal enrollment.

Acquiring Indian land was a goal of many of the government's policies, and encouraging intermarriage was yet another tool toward that purpose. An Indian woman who received allotment land as the head of household, if she married a European, would find her title granted to the man at the end of the twenty-five-year trust period. Even the 1856 Lake Pepin Half-Breed Reserve list was signed by the illiterate Louis on Rosalie's behalf.

As the number of mixed-blood children raised under the influence of European values continued to increase, they began to exert more influence within the tribes, some of them encouraging treaty negotiations that resulted in the signing away of traditional lands. In 1849, after Minnesota Territory was organized, the new governor, Alexander Ramsey, made a priority of negotiating a treaty with the Dakota Indians for the land they controlled, which covered most of the southern half of what would become Minnesota. As Rosalie was giving birth to her third child in 1851, Lillia, whose godparent would be the prosperous trader Louis Robert, Dakota tribes were about to sign the treaties of Traverse des Sioux and Mendota, relinquishing all of their land west of the Mississippi River. In exchange for 7.5 cents per acre, $30,000 for schools, and a controversial payment of traders' debts, the tribes agreed to move to a reservation consisting of a twenty-mile-wide strip of land on either side of the Minnesota River.

The treaty was strongly supported by Henry Sibley, who had traded with the Dakota for twenty years, and by powerful mixed-blood families, without whom the treaty might never have been signed. This only served to deepen the hostility between traditional and mixed-blood Indians.

The Dakota tribes were understandably reluctant to leave their traditional hunting grounds for the reservation, especially when promised annuities were late in coming and generally amounted to far less than what had been promised. By 1853, as Rosalie and Louis welcomed their fourth child, Helene, to the family, most of the tribes had moved, but they continued to hunt in the winter and return to their old villages, even as white settlers moved in and claimed the land as their own. The Wacouta band returned from a winter hunt one year to find their bark houses burned by the new residents of Red Wing. In 1857, the St. Paul *Daily Times* summed up the general attitude of white settlers: "But one sentiment appeared to inspire almost the entire population, and this was, the total annihilation of the Indian race within their borders." By 1858, the tribes had sold their ten-mile strip on the north side of the river, and suddenly Louis and Rosalie were no longer living on reservation land.

One of the early white settlers in the area was Helen Mar Tarble, a teenage bride who had arrived with her new husband in 1857. The first night of their arrival at the Lower Agency, they

> camped on the land of a Frenchman named LaCroix, who was married to a squaw. They invited me into their house, but I was afraid of the repulsive looking squaw, and I implored my husband to go back with me; I told him I could not stay there. . . . We staid at LaCroix's three days. Mr. LaCroix would come out to the wagon and ask me into his kitchen, but I was afraid of his squaw and did not dare to go. Then they would both come, and she would tell me as best she could to come and cook on her stove. They tried to help and comfort me and were very kind. I felt sorry to go from them, yet I did not get over my fear of that squaw. To me then she was the most repulsive looking woman I ever beheld.

I wanted to rip Tarble's face off.

Once the area was opened to settlers, Louis was one of the first to make a claim on the land where he had built his family's home. He managed to acquire a fair amount of land and some measure of prosperity; the town of Morton was originally built on land he owned. He may have been helped, in part, by his friendship with Louis Robert. His obituary in 1874, however, indicates that by the time of his death, he had also managed to give his prosperity away, a man who was a good relative to his Indian family. Louis was described as "generous to a fault and this was the reason why he died quite without means, even though at times he had a richly blessed living." Or as my Swedish relatives would have said with mournful shakes of their heads, he "gave away the store." A point of pride in Indian culture, in which a person's character is measured by his or her generosity, but something of a catastrophe among the Scandinavians.

This difference in attitude toward material possessions was one of the most rancorous, divisive issues between the two cultures. Missionaries and Indian agents despaired of ever "civilizing" a people who insisted on giving away their possessions. They tried to forbid "giveaway" ceremonies and to instill the value of working toward individual profit and accumulating property rather than sharing it. This cultural generosity was fundamental to Dakota people, and it reflected their belief that wealth was demonstrated by how much was given away, not in how much was kept. Sitting Bull summed up this difference by saying, "The white man knows how to make everything, but he does not know how to distribute it."

Rosalie disappeared after Louis LaCroix died in 1874 at Big Stone Lake near the South Dakota border. Historical records tend to ignore women in general, and Indian women in particular, extending a layer of invisibility in accordance with their status. I could not find any record of Rosalie's birth, baptism, or death. Yet I was also beginning to feel that Rosalie's story was the one that most needed to be pulled out from the shadows of history. Twenty-six years of marriage to a white trader, exposure to shocking racism from white settlers, and her experience seeking refuge at Fort Ridgely during the war must have affected Rosalie deeply. After Louis died, where had she gone and why?

Three of Rosalie's sons were living on the Sisseton reservation at the time of the 1880 census. Fred was a thirty-two-year-old carpenter, and his youngest brother, Oliver, was a nineteen-year-old musician who lived with him. Louis was a thirty-year-old farmer. Both Fred and Louis had acquired 160 acres of allotment land through the 1867 treaty that established the reservation. The first white babies in Renville County were now being counted as Indian; none of them could read or write. Fred also used his Indian birth order name, Cuske Tanke, or eldest son. This was the only time following Rosalie's marriage certificate that I saw an Indian name used by the LaCroix. The act of being given an Indian name was so important and intrinsic to Dakota culture that the absence of those names in the family revealed much about their cultural values. This single exception was all the more striking because of Fred's service as a Renville Ranger.

After a long, fruitless search for any information about Rosalie, I decided in desperation to make a trip to the Sisseton reservation. After a patient search of their probate records, I found it: a tiny bit of information that made this 500-mile trip worth my time and gas. A rancorous dispute had arisen following Louis's death about whether he had adopted two children according to "Indian" custom or legally in terms of inheritance. The dispute required testimony from a number of people, including Thomas A. Robertson, a scout in the 1862 war. As a result of this transcript, I discovered that Rosalie had lived briefly with her son, Louis, in 1877 and that she had worked in the Sisseton Agency school. I knew that she had moved to the reservation after Louis died, along with her children. I wondered if she had learned to read or write, and what work she did at the school. Had she ever remarried or rejoined her own band? These are questions that I may never be able to answer.

Later that afternoon, I stopped at St. Matthew's cemetery just outside the town of Veblen, twenty miles north of Sisseton, hoping to find Rosalie's grave. After opening the gate, I found myself in the middle of a cemetery that had two distinct sides with a path running down the middle. When the cemetery was first established, whites had been buried on the left with monuments and stone markers, while Indians had been buried on the right under plain white crosses among a few scattered monuments. The custom had continued, maintained by the tendency of families to be buried together in the same section. I did not find any of the graves for Louis, Jr., Fred, or Rosalie. Instead, I found other LaCroix family members buried on the Indian side, including one of Louis, Jr.'s sons, William. Next to his marker was an empty place for his wife, Marion. No old graves appeared in this cemetery, so I knew that there must be another place, most likely a cemetery forgotten by anyone but the elders. I had no idea whom to ask, except to call Marion LaCroix, the unburied wife of William. After finding her phone number, I called her and said that I was a distant relative. While contacting strangers is a gamble in terms of finding information, I'm always optimistic that each new contact may be willing to share stories and old photos and, in the best of all worlds, reveal where my relatives are buried.

"I think we're related through the LaCroix family," was my hopeful introduction.

"I know there's LaCroixs all over," she said flatly. "There's some down in Santee, some in California. We don't know that we're related to any of them." Her voice, unmistakably Indian in rhythm, conveyed a distinct lack of interest in the question.

"You are a LaCroix by marriage?"

"Yeah."

In the background I could hear a voice asking if she had eaten the last pork chop for breakfast. I was not family to her, no matter how many years she had been married into the family. Family follows its own blood line, and her connection to the LaCroix family had been buried, twice. I was not disappointed, accustomed as I had become to the dead ends that are part of the search, seeing them not so much as obstacles but as the peculiar form that information sometimes takes. Even in the absence of learning the location of Rosalie's grave, there is knowledge to be gained. Was there irony as well, that the reservation LaCroixs refused any connection to their extended family?

But at least I knew that Rosalie had moved here with her children after her husband died, that Fred and Louis were enrolled in the Sisseton tribe, and that they knew the Renville family and

Thomas A. Robertson. By choosing to live here, on the reservation led by chief Gabriel Renville, the mixed blood who refused to speak English and who maintained his cultural identity, they, too, may have resisted any further absorption into white culture. It was no coincidence that the LaCroixs who stayed on this reservation still buried their family on the Indian side of the cemetery.

20 *Minnesota's Legacy*

AUGUST 2001
Lower Sioux Agency, Minnesota

On the land where the Dakota used to collect their annuities at the Lower Sioux Agency, tourists now wander through exhibits in a modern historical building staffed by people who are mildly obsessed with the 1862 war. Outside, small wooden signs mark where the traders' stores used to be. Familiar, well-known names like Andrew Myrick, François La Bathe, and Louis Robert are all that remain of buildings that were destroyed by fire.

Standing next to me was John LaBatte, a descendent of François La Bathe, whose family had been neighbors of the LaCroixs in the 1860s. I had been introduced to John at the Minnesota Historical Society a month earlier. He was also researching his family's history around this same area. As we talked that day at the historical society office, I sat idly leafing through the pages of my genealogy charts, when I suddenly realized that his ancestor had been married to my great-grandmother's sister, making us shirttail cousins. François La Bathe had lived in the mixed-blood community near the LaCroix family until he moved to the Lower Agency and built his store.

Four generations later, John and I were walking together across the same land where Louis and François had most likely traded goods, on ground where François lay dying after the fighting broke out. A remarkable coincidence, at least, that led us to be standing here together. Or perhaps there was something unresolved about this period in history, something left unsaid about our families' experience during the war that had drawn us both to this place.

More signs pointed to the Episcopal and Presbyterian churches, the warehouse, the government building, and the blacksmith's shop that had once stood nearby. I could see the traces of François La Bathe's log home, where a hastily appointed five-man military tribunal had administered frontier justice 140 years earlier.

As I stood near the outline of the traders' stores, feeling the sun warm on my face, I could hear the first shots fired, smell the sharp bite of gunpowder and the acrid smoke of a new fire. Across a field of empty grass, François La Bathe had been shot in his store on the morning of August 18. Andrew Myrick had been shot while trying to escape through an upstairs window, while his Dakota wife Nancy hid behind the door with a knife in one hand and her baby, Mary, in the other.

Another sign pointed down the hill toward the old landing for the Redwood Ferry, where a Frenchman, Oliver Martell, had helped people escape across the river. I decided to walk down the hill, despite the intense heat already building at mid-morning, while John chose to remain in the air-conditioned museum.

It was a steep decline toward the river, and I was the only one that day who thought the hike was worth the effort. Or perhaps they, too, had heard the rumors that there were cougars again prowling the woods. I started at a brisk pace but was soon slowed by my difficulty in breathing humid air. I failed to see a large spiderweb strung between the trees, and its soft, sticky filaments enveloped my face and hair. A feeling of near panic made it even harder to breathe. The layer of sweat that was now accumulating on my neck seemed to trap the tiny black gnats that formed a cloud about my head, moving with me as I hiked. I continued all the way to the landing.

The woods were dense near the river, having been little disturbed over the years. The water swirled past over stumps of fallen trees whose remaining branches reminded me of upflung arms, my imagination beginning to overreact to the almost unnatural silence of these woods. I glanced once, twice over my shoulder, wishing to be sure that I was alone—or at least not someone's prey.

I stood near the water's edge and took pictures of the not-too-distant shore where the ferry used to land near the road that led to Fort Ridgely. The mouth of Birch Coulee or LaCroix Creek was also near the ferry landing. I imagined how Captain Marsh and his forty-six men, come to quell the uprising, had arrived on the opposite side of the river, no doubt sweating profusely from the same August heat that now sent rivulets of sweat down my sides. They found the flat-bottomed ferryboat conveniently waiting to take them across the river. Standing where I now stood had been a Dakota man named White Dog, who supposedly asked the soldiers to come across and hold a council. When the soldiers did not move, a shot was fired and Indians sprung up from the brush all around them, killing twelve soldiers immediately.

The silence that filled these woods was palpable, laden with reverberations of this old tragedy. I had felt this same heaviness at the site of the Wounded Knee massacre, on the land where the Battle of Little Big Horn took place, and in Mankato, where thirty-eight men had been hung following the 1862 war. As the land absorbed the blood of the men, women, and children who were killed, it formed a crust, a blend of dirt, blood, spirit, bone, terror, and pain, so that grief hovered above these areas like the shimmer of heat on a blacktop highway.

In such places, the decades that have passed since the massacre have not at all diminished the sense that the land itself, even the river, have been victims of this tragedy. These are literally the wounds in Minnesota's history that still lie close to the surface, even if their immediate details are no longer remembered by the descendants of those who were here. I've heard it said that "Minnesota nice" is nothing more than a thin veil across a layer of barely repressed racism, and sometimes I wonder if that accusation has its roots in the memories of places like this one. The details may not be remembered, but the visceral impression of grief and rage and terror has been imprinted in the bodies of all who were here, a legacy that has been passed invisibly from one generation to the next. Here on this land, the destinies of hundreds of white families and the entire Dakota people were changed forever.

21 *Through Dakota Eyes*

OCTOBER 2001
Cannon Falls, Minnesota

About thirteen miles downriver from the Lower Sioux Agency, Fort Ridgely overlooks the ravines that surround it, offering a clear view of the Minnesota River valley below. Beneath the surface of this historic site, archeologists have found evidence that the Dakota lived here before the fort was built. In the center of the grounds a monument has been erected to honor the soldiers and armed civilians who defended the fort in 1862. Louis LaCroix is listed as an armed civilian, and his oldest son, Fred, as a private in the Renville Rangers. Missing from that list is Augustin Frenier; Rosalie is not named as one of the heroic women who helped defend the fort.

I walked around the crumbled remains of the two-foot-thick stone walls that outline the barracks where the women and children were gathered for their protection. Stepping inside, I stood facing toward the valley where they knew the Dakota attack must come.

After I visited the fort, images of the Dakota War began to haunt my thoughts and even my dreams. I was tormented by the thought of Rosalie taking refuge at Fort Ridgely: Rosalie with her dark skin surrounded by whites whose husbands or wives or children had just been killed by Dakota warriors. I felt pregnant, a woman heavy with impending birth.

I decided to spend a few days at a friend's farmhouse in Cannon Falls, hoping to find relief from these images by turning them into a story about Rosalie and her experience. The farmhouse was perched on the side of a hill that sloped down to the sheep barn and then abruptly fell away to a steep, wood-lined ravine. A long, stubbled field separated the house from its nearest neighbor. It seemed like the perfect place; the Wahpekutes had originally settled near the mouth of the Cannon River. This was Rosalie's land, possibly even her birthplace.

I read about the war, studied the personal narratives of Dakota people who survived the conflict, reread old newspaper accounts, and looked at photographs I had taken at the Lower Sioux Agency and Fort Ridgely. For three days I read, slept, and waited to begin writing.

One morning I woke too early, well before dawn, and lay there listening for the sound that brought me out of a deep sleep. The bed faced an east window on the second floor, with the roof slanting at sharp angles in the corners of the room.

As I lay there, I heard slow footsteps and the creak of a wood floor. Immediately alert, with adrenalin beginning to prickle the skin on my arms, I hoped that these slow, almost dragging footsteps and the quiet groan of old wood were nothing more than an animal on the roof. Yet it sounded more like an old man or woman walking with painful care across the kitchen floor and into the living room, the sound carried upward through the vent in my bedroom floor.

My grandmother Rosalie, perhaps, feeling her story rise up like the light that brightened my window, now that her place in our family's history would be remembered? Perhaps she was impatient for me to begin to write and so she walked, knowing that I would waken and hear her call.

After several long minutes, the footsteps stopped as suddenly as they had begun. I listened to the common sounds of dawn in the country, hearing nothing more ominous than the far-off cry of a rooster.

I knew it would be painful to imagine Rosalie's experience during the war. Even though 140 years have passed, the Dakota War seems as fresh, as relevant, and as frightening to me as it must have felt in 1862. The daily newspapers are filled with news of the U.S. invasion of Afghanistan, of suicide bombings and the rumblings of war in the Middle East, stories whose roots bear striking parallels to 1862. Religious intolerance, greed, and imperialism continue to fuel hate and violence, just as they sparked a war in Minnesota. Perhaps Rosalie comes to serve as a guide and a guardian.

There are strong parallels between Rosalie and my mother, Lucille, similarities that connect their lives despite the generations between them. They both married white traders (one in fur, one in retail) and raised their children according to European values. Both women experienced enormous pressure to adapt to white culture, followed by a traumatic moment in their lives that greatly influenced their decisions when a choice was offered: the illusion of safety in the white world or the uncertainty of living in a culture under constant, insidious attack. In those moments, the choice offered by circumstance may not have seemed like a choice at all.

Rosalie's marriage to a French Canadian, followed by the 1862 war, was one of the first great rifts in our family's Dakota identity. Her marriage sent our bloodline spinning off into another culture, creating the first generation of mixed-blood children, who had to balance the often opposing values of two cultures. The pain she must have felt at Fort Ridgely, the pain of the entire Dakota nation at war not only with whites but also with each other, had nowhere to go, no resolution, no possibility of healing for generations. It rambled along, like a mutated gene, visiting my grandmothers and my aunts and finally landing in my mother's lap.

There is a Lakota saying, *Tohan mate sni ehatan,* which means "As long as I'm alive." Severt Young Bear explains in his book *Standing in the Light: A Lakota Way of Seeing* that a family's history, its name, its unique identity only survive as long as there is someone to remember them. Writing the book was his way of maintaining his family's name and history "as long as I'm alive." His words explained to me why it was so important to recover these stories, to learn who my family was, and to share the process of what it meant to travel back in time and rebuild relationships. This was the answer to the question raised at the Journey Museum—why we need to know our family history. I, too, have a responsibility, for as long as I'm alive, not only to maintain my family's history but also to help shape it for future generations.

The next day I called my friend Kate, a poet who had slept in my room the night before I arrived in Cannon Falls. I described the footsteps I had heard and told her about Rosalie. She sounded surprised and said that she had dreamed that night of an Indian woman who stood alone, aloof, and not easily approached. She wore a red strip of cloth braided in her dark hair.

There was no doubt in my mind that Rosalie had come home.

A few months later, at the tender age of forty-seven, I told my parents that I planned to marry my partner, Jim Denomie, whom I had been dating for six years. I invited them out for dinner and we chatted about my plans for a simple ceremony at a restaurant in St. Paul, with my brother Dave playing music. My father cleared his throat as if he had something to say.

"This is a big step for you," he said. I was immediately alert, unaccustomed to hearing my father make reflective statements. He has a generous heart and a great love of entertaining people with his jokes, but he is a man of blunt speech, not insight. I was curious to hear where this was going to lead.

"Getting married to Jim is a big step," he continued. "After all, he's Indian and you're white." He said nothing more and began to push pasta noodles onto his fork, as if avoiding eye contact.

My mother and I exchanged a look, but we said nothing.

Why, I wondered, did he feel the need to tell me that I was white? Maybe he was reminding me that I was also descended from a long line of Swedish settlers who had worked hard to give their children better lives than their own, regardless of the cost. That my comfortable life growing up in a suburb carried a price tag, an obligation to maintain the world as he knew it, where white history overshadowed everything. Forget the past, he might have been saying, the past that my mother had tried to ignore, burying it the same way our chihuahua buried the sweaters she knit for him, a trace of yarn still visible above the snow. Or maybe my father was just reminding me of who I was, in his eyes.

As we planned our wedding, Jim and I asked a friend of his, Chuck Robertson, an elder who is both Dakota and Ojibwe, to perform the spiritual part of the ceremony. I knew him slightly, having met him years earlier when Jim had painted a backdrop for one of his plays.

Chuck invited us for dinner to talk about the wedding ceremony. His Irish wife, Cathy, served perfectly cooked steaks while we talked about Chuck's most recent play. After dinner, Chuck excused himself, saying he wanted to show me something.

He came back holding the book *Through Dakota Eyes,* the collection of firsthand testimonials from Dakota people about the 1862 war. His copy was worn and had obviously been read many times. Thumbing through it quickly, he opened it to the page about Thomas A. Robertson, the mixed blood who had testified for the LaCroix family at Sisseton and had been a courier during the 1862 war.

"That's my great-grandfather," Chuck said.

Of course it was. I could only laugh, delighted, surprised, and a bit spooked, all at once. At the risk of reading too much into the obvious synchronicity of this meeting, he was the third person, starting with John LaBatte, whom I had met recently whose families had had relationships with my family dating back at least 140 years. A few months earlier, a volunteer at the historical society had casually asked what I was working on after seeing the Renville County History lying open on my table. When I told him briefly about the LaCroix family, he looked startled and said, "My great-grandfather bought that land from Louis LaCroix." His family still lives there today. Maybe these "coincidences" simply meant that my eyes were open now, open to the possibility that there were many of us whose lives would intersect around the 1862 war. Perhaps the time had come for this story to be told so that our generation could grieve for all that had been lost in 1862 and the years afterward.

In the next few months, Chuck and I continued to discuss the Dakota War and our relatives, sharing a mutual fascination with this history. Occasionally he sent me some of his writing about the prisoners at Davenport or Fort Snelling. In his notes, he called me Dakota-Wi, or Dakota woman. He also talked about what it meant to be a mixed-blood person, how he accepts all of his heritage: Dakota, Ojibwe, and German.

"You have to make a choice," Jim told me when we talked about the difficulty of juggling two cultures as a mixed blood. A choice, meaning that even when you accept your mixed heritage, you have to choose where to stand, and you have to accept responsibility for that decision. If we live out our convictions in the choices we make, then you have to ask yourself: What does my life stand for?

One afternoon in October, I opened a flyer announcing the Dakota Commemorative March. By the time I had finished reading it, I knew that I would be part of it.

22 *Dakota Homecoming*

NOVEMBER 7, 2002
Lower Sioux Reservation, Minnesota

At sunrise the sky was bright and cloudless, the air still sharp and cold, and the sun had not yet melted a thin layer of frost that covered the grass. My brother Dave and I had spent the night at the Lower Sioux reservation casino just outside of Morton, Minnesota. With little information beyond what we had read in a flyer a month earlier, we had come to be part of the first-ever Dakota Commemorative March. We would be joining a group of strangers who had organized a 150-mile walk from the Lower Sioux reservation to Fort Snelling to honor the mostly women, children, and elders who had been forced to make this journey 140 years earlier.

After stopping once to get directions to the community building, Dave and I walked into a windowless basement and paused near the door, getting a feel for the room and the people who had already gathered there.

The center of the basement was crowded with a long table filled with metal trays of food donated by the casino—bacon, sausage, eggs, sweet rolls, orange juice, and coffee. About two dozen people were scattered at tables around the room. Almost immediately, one of the March organizers, Angela Cavender Wilson, came up to greet us with a warm handshake. Her younger son, Sage, stood close to his mother's side while we talked. Angela told us that she and her three children had flown in a few days earlier from Arizona, where she teaches American Indian history at Arizona State University. She waved a hand at the food table,

urging us to eat. We would leave following a short prayer ceremony after breakfast.

Angela's father, Chris Mato Nunpa, was the next person to
come and shake hands with us. He taught Indigenous Nations and
Dakota Studies at Southwest Minnesota State University in Mar-
shall, not far from Morton. He had taken on the job of organizing
the practical side of the March, finding places for the marchers to
sleep each night and asking for donations of food from various
tribes and organizations. He said later, with his quick laugh, that
his Indian name ought to be changed to Worry-Wart.

"Who are you here with?" he asked.

"Ourselves," was my reply, bringing a laugh from Chris.

"No," he explained. "I mean, do you have Dakota relatives at
the Lower Sioux?" He was trying to understand our connection to
the March.

"Our great-great-grandmother, Rosalie Marpiya Mase, or Iron
Cloud, lived across the river from the Lower Agency when the
1862 war broke out," I said. I didn't explain that she was not part
of the march. Chris nodded his head, pleased to hear that another Dakota family had returned to the area for this event. He
introduced us to several other people at one of the tables and
urged us to eat, then turned to greet new arrivals.

I heard that question about relatives many times on that first
day and every day that followed. We were all intensely interested
in how people were related, how they connected to the Lower and
Upper Sioux communities, what reservation they were enrolled
in, and whether they had relatives on the original march. A few
families, like Angela's, still had stories from the 1862 march that
had been passed down between generations. In a large group of
strangers, Indian people use family relationship like a compass, as
a way of steering through complex connections and acknowledging family ties, no matter how distant.

After breakfast we gathered outside in a large circle, about
forty or so people who ranged in age from five to eighty-five. The
sun was beginning to warm the air, but my breath still formed a
cold cloud as I waited, arms folded against my body for warmth.

One of the men slowly walked around the circle carrying a bowl of burning sage, as Chris Mato Nunpa welcomed us. He reminded us how our ancestors had left the Lower Sioux reservation 140 years earlier, when almost the entire nation of Dakota people was imprisoned or evicted from Minnesota following the end of the Dakota War.

> On November 7, 1862, a four-mile train of mostly women and children was forced to march to the concentration camps at Fort Snelling. Many of our people died on this trip. The townspeople from Henderson, New Ulm, and Sleepy Eye threw bricks as they passed by, they threw stones, one woman even threw boiling water.
>
> Some people ask why we need to remember this, why we can't just let it go. The march has never been acknowledged for the tragic event that it was. It's been covered up and forgotten. It's time for the Dakota people to remember their ancestors, to grieve for their family who were part of this march. This used to be Dakota land. It was all taken away from us. When you allow these things to be covered up, that's part of colonization.

As Chris explained later during the March, colonization meant that not only had Europeans stolen ancestral lands and sought to dismantle Dakota culture, but that Dakotas themselves had absorbed these attitudes over time. If historic trauma occurs that is never resolved, never acknowledged or forgiven, then the act of closing one's eyes to it is a form of collusion with the colonizer. Even if the event occurred 140 years earlier.

Up until this point, no one had explained our family's experience as part of a broad historical process: Christianity, boarding schools, land allotment, and blood quantum were all persuasive tools in assimilating families like ours. My first reaction was one of relief that our family experience was shared by many others— followed quickly by a return of the simmering anger I had felt ever since reading Tarble's description of Rosalie. I was beginning to understand how abstract concepts like assimilation or colonization can raise a feeling of rage when applied to my own family.

After a closing prayer spoken in Dakota, we formed a loose group that moved slowly down the long driveway leading to the road. Angela's eighty-five-year-old grandmother, Naomi Cavender, from Santee, Nebraska, led the group briefly, pushing her great-grandson's stroller a short distance until her strength gave out. She traveled the rest of the week in a van behind the marchers. The group was led by Leo Omani and his "red pony," a vehicle of mature years that Leo and his nephew, Gerald Standing, had driven from their reservation in Saskatchewan, Canada. It was Leo who first had the idea that the women and children who had marched in 1862 needed to be remembered and grieved by their descendents.

We walked along the shoulder of the highway behind an eagle staff of thirty-eight feathers that commemorated the thirty-eight warriors hung at Mankato. After a mile, the "red pony" stopped and Leo climbed out carrying a three-foot wood stake with a red prayer tie near the top and the names of two of the original marchers written on each side in Dakota. Leo asked one of the elders to translate the names. After we listened to the names, he began searching the ravine for something to pound the stake into the ground.

"Aha," Leo cried, holding a large rock above his head. "A Canadian hammer!" He pounded the stake swiftly into the ground. One by one, each of the marchers placed a pinch of tobacco around the stake, pausing a moment in silent prayer.

The March had begun.

Each day we walked at least twenty miles, following approximately the same route as the original marchers. We placed a stake at each mile for the entire 150 miles of the March. Community and student groups donated food and an organization in each town provided free shelter each night. The magnificent three-seat rolling toilet that followed along behind the group, complete with stalls, wallpaper, and piped-in music, was provided by the Lower Sioux Tribal Council.

After a long day of walking, we hobbled into a church or

school gymnasium, sat wearily at the tables, and ate supper. Shoes were immediately loosened. When it came time to fill plates with food, many people moved to the table on slow, stiff legs and sore feet. After dinner, marchers offered their stories about their families' experience in the original march or during the war.

One evening, Angela explained how the March was conceived as a way of understanding how the social problems that Indian communities struggle with—alcoholism, depression, suicide, abuse—are a consequence of colonization. "Our thinking was that we need to do some healing ourselves and we need to come to terms with some of these injustices. We need to come to terms with the violence that was perpetrated against us because I think many of us today carry a great deal of what we might call histori- cal grief, that pain that hasn't been reconciled for all of the injus- tices perpetrated against us."

Sleeping mats were unrolled on the floor for those who stayed each night, falling quickly into a deep, exhausted slumber. Each morning began early with breakfast, prayers, sometimes a pipe ceremony, and then the group returned to the last wood stake that had been placed the night before.

We walked through the towns of Sleepy Eye, New Ulm, and Mankato, names made infamous by townspeople who channeled their own grief into murderous rage. But this March was peaceful, passing through these towns without incident. The route became more difficult as the long caravan of marchers and cars left be- hind the bucolic back roads near the Lower Sioux reservation and began walking on the shoulders of increasingly busy highways.

After the first warm day of marching, when the afternoon sun still felt like late summer, the weather soon reverted to fall. By the fourth day, arriving in Henderson after long hours buffeted by the high winds that swirled behind each passing truck, the group marched silently for the last hour into a bitter, cold sleet.

On the morning of the seventh and last day of the March, I woke at 5:00 AM, my hip aching so that it hurt to stand, hurt to walk to my kitchen. In the two days that I had not walked with the March because of work commitments, after leaving the group at a community center in Henderson, the pain had grown worse. At night I fell asleep and dreamed of the eagle staff moving steadily down the road ahead of the group, my legs following behind with strong, sure steps. In the morning I woke tired, my knees sore, my hip aching. I drank my coffee, burned sage with a prayer for strength for the marchers, swallowed four ibuprofen, and drove through the pre-dawn morning to the Little Six Casino in Prior Lake.

The group had grown larger with each passing day as more marchers arrived from the Santee reservation in Nebraska, the Sisseton reservation in South Dakota, and reservations across Canada, where Dakota people had fled in 1862 rather than risk hanging or prison. This March was their homecoming, the return of the Dakota so many generations later to ancestral land.

After breakfast, we regrouped at mile marker 92 on Highway 13, where the previous day's march had ended. The woman who offered the morning prayer wept as she spoke. Already the mood of the group had begun to shift, feeling the weight of six days of remembering, of sharing stories with other descendents, combined with the sense that we were about to end this long, exhausting journey. The March was approaching what had been the prison camp at Fort Snelling, the winter home where many more of the original marchers had died of disease.

We walked along the shoulder of the highway with red prayer ties braided in the women's hair, tied to the antennas of a long line of cars and vans, wound around the arms of the men who carried the eagle staff at the head of our procession. The wind was strong and cold that morning, rising up to meet this group with its own challenge, the air whipped by the passage of fast-moving cars and trucks. I walked alongside Dottie Whipple, a retired nurse, whose lighthearted conversation helped pass the miles quickly.

We crossed freeway ramps by stopping traffic. My brother Dave and Scott Wilson acted as modern day "dog soldiers," protecting the passage of this ungainly caravan. They wore orange plastic vests and stood at the top of the freeway entrances, waving their arms at cars that hit their brakes suddenly, surprised by the unexpected presence of a long line of people walking along the highway. Some drivers seemed to clench in frustration at having their morning commutes made even longer, their fingers tapping the steering wheel. Others honked and waved in support, waiting patiently for the long line to cross safely. We saw a large group of schoolchildren who lined up across the street and waved, all of them excited about the March passing by.

After we had walked about ten miles, we stopped for lunch, which was spread across the trunk and hood of a large car. Still standing, we ate bologna sandwiches, chocolate chip cookies, and apples. News of the March had attracted a reporter who interviewed Naomi Cavender. Knowing that Naomi was from Santee, Nebraska, I stood and listened while they talked. When the reporter was finished, I asked Naomi if she knew the LaCroix family. "Oh sure," she said, her eyes lighting up with recognition. I told her that my grandmother Maude had been born on Santee. She wrinkled her forehead at that name, saying she didn't think Maude was in her time. I asked about Oliver and Jenny LaCroix, about Clarence LaCroix, who had died in the past decade, and she nodded her head—"Yes, yes, I knew them." I thanked her and made my way back to the marchers who were once again gathering behind the red pony. It was a smaller group walking after lunch and we joked that the others needed a nap as the group of cars following us continued to grow. We also had a second eagle staff at the front of the line, carried by Bob Brown from Mendota.

I walked several miles with Joanne, a young woman who was studying Dakota in a two-year immersion program sponsored by the Shakopee community. She and the others in her program had heard that morning that the March was on Highway 13, so they jumped into the reservation van and came down to walk with us. Originally they had intended to walk part of the day and return for a meeting at 2:30. When I saw her again in the afternoon, she said they had decided to walk the entire distance. That happened often on the March. People who came for a few hours or a single day ended up returning again and again, compelled by a force that none of us could name. My brother walked with a broken toe six of the seven days, staying home only to make phone calls to find the marchers a place to stay on the last night. He had also made a name for himself on the first day when he carried the eagle staff at such a brisk pace that the other marchers had to walk fast to keep up with him. Later he would say what all of us had felt, that we were filled with an energy that made walking twenty miles seem, if not easy, then very attainable.

I also walked next to a man who wore a sky blue jacket with the hood pulled up so that I could only see his face when he turned his head. After I learned that he was from Santee, I asked if he knew Willard Mackey, my good-natured tour guide across the reservation. "Willard passed away," he said. We walked together for a long time in silence.

Sometimes when we stopped to place a stake, it broke and had to be mended with one of the red ties. Leo said that this was a symbol for the March itself: something that had been broken by the original march was being mended. When marchers recognized the names of a relative who had been part of the original march, they stood near the stake, wiping away tears.

That afternoon when we stopped again to place yet another stake at one of the mile markers, Leo said, "This one is easy to understand, no translation is needed, as it is not an Indian name." When it was my turn to say a prayer and place tobacco at the base of the stake, I read the names: Narcisse and Louise Frenier. Grandmother Jenny's great-uncle and another relative. I felt an electric shock of recognition travel down the length of my arms, all thoughts of prayer momentarily suspended. These names belonged to my family.

In that single moment, all the years of research that I had done about my family, about the 1862 war and the removal of the Dakota people, all of the reading, the writing, and the interviews, the re-imagined stories, even the walking and the hearing of names of the original marchers—it all came together in a single, overwhelming feeling of grief. Where I had felt compassion for the other marchers and a strong interest in the history, suddenly it became personal. It was *my* family who had been abused as they passed through the towns of New Ulm, Henderson, and Mankato. It had been *my* relatives who were hit by bricks, stones, and scalding water, who had been spat on, taunted, hated. I was stunned by this realization, watching as each one in the group took turns offering tobacco and prayers to my relatives, to my family. I stood there and wept.

An hour later I was walking next to Clifford Canku, a spiritual leader from Sisseton. We exchanged stories, telling about our relatives and what had drawn us to be part of this March. He asked, "Has it made an impact on you?" I told him how I had just read my relatives' names a few miles back and had felt, for the first time, a powerful sense of grief for the original marchers, that in mourning for my own family, I had felt the March become personal as well as for the Dakota people.

Clifford thought for a moment and then told me we are all part of the collective unconscious, and the people's connection to it is growing stronger, partly because of events like the March. When people come back to their heritage, he explained, when they learn their language, when they march to reconcile a part of history that has never been acknowledged, then they are slowly putting together the pieces of their lives, like a puzzle.

A few miles later, I carried tobacco to the next stake and recognized the names of Thomas A. Robertson and Angus Robertson, his brother. As I placed tobacco for Chuck's relatives, I remembered our location so that I could call him later and tell him where to find the stake.

By midafternoon, when we had marched almost fourteen miles, we turned onto old Highway 13, also known as the Sibley Memorial Highway. At one of the last mile markers before we reached the Mendota Bridge and crossed to Fort Snelling, Leo stood in front of the group and announced that it was time for the men who had led the March with the eagle staffs to step aside.

"This March is to acknowledge the women and children and elders who made this journey, and they need to go ahead of the men. They are the givers of life," he said. "The men will walk beside them and behind them."

As the men moved in silence to walk along both sides of our small band of women, a palpable wave of grief settled in. The history that we had re-created began to blur the distinction between past and present, and my sense that we were not alone on this journey grew even stronger. I was near the back of the group of women and children, and I could see how we had been transformed by Leo's words. Angela Cavender Wilson, the woman who was the heart of the March, one of the primary organizers and the only person to walk the entire 150 miles, became the lightning rod for the dark feelings that washed over the women. She was the first to begin weeping with deep, shuddering sobs, her head bowed while she continued to walk with her arms wrapped tightly around two of her children. One of the women waved an eagle feather around her head, while others patted her gently on her back. Gerald asked Dave to stay near her, burning sweet grass as they walked.

Clifford also filled a tiny bowl with sage and moved through the group, stopping briefly to allow each woman to wave the smoke into her face, hair, and breath. It became difficult to continue walking as my limbs grew heavy and weak, and I was filled with an absolute sense of despair that deepened the closer we came to the bridge that led us to the prison camp below. The pain in my left hip had returned, and my entire right arm and shoulder ached as if I had been carrying something I could not set down, a baby perhaps, or the weight of an elder leaning on my arm.

As we continued to walk, it was as if the pavement beneath the women's feet began to fade and disappear, the rigid layer of tar and gravel slowly giving in to the prairie beneath. With each step we moved further back into the past, until long-stemmed grasses now bent beneath the hems of the women's long skirts. We began to move in our own private landscape, all of us marching together in the same dream. The wind traded the fumes of truck exhaust and fast-food grease for the rich scent of leaves decaying on moist

Apistoka, a Dakota woman held at the Fort Snelling prison camp, winter 1862

earth, crushed by the slow rolling of wagon wheels. The fields had been turned under for fall, a thick layer of pungent manure spread across the black soil, its neatly furrowed rows a testament to the white farmers who now owned it, who subdued it with their plows and horses. Even the land had lost its freedom, lost its wild mane of prairie.

The men disappeared, banished to the prison at Mankato, leaving the women guarded by a long string of soldiers on horses. Our small group swelled until it stretched into four miles of women and children walking, with a few wagons that carried the elders, the meager possessions we were allowed to bring, the children who were too young to walk, and those who were already ill. The long train of people and wagons snaked slowly behind us all the way to the horizon, pointing the way back to the land that had been stripped from the Dakota people.

We had been forced to march over twenty miles each day for seven days, and sometimes one of the women stumbled, her legs giving way in exhaustion. "Get up," was the order, as a rifle was pointed at the prostrate figure on the ground. "Get up or plan to stay here," the soldier said with an ugly laugh, his small eyes lingering on the hip of the young woman who bent quickly to help, to pull her aunt to her feet, to whisper in her ear that she must, she must get up quickly, "We will rest soon." Her aunt looked up, and even I could see the surrender in her soul, her willingness to go no further, to have her life end beneath the broad sky of the prairie she had always known, leaving her bones unburied, her memory lost to her family. The old woman rose slowly and painfully, her life now a gift to her niece. She leaned her weight on the girl's arm while the crowd of women flowed slowly around them, murmuring, "Come, Auntie," patting her arm and her shoulder as they walked past on sore, swollen feet.

The sky was gray and heavy with snow, the wind gusting in swirls of leaves that danced around their legs, as if mocking them, knowing that some of these women would never dance again. Women pulled their blankets tightly around their shoulders to keep the wind from finding their hearts, from tearing their children from their grasp, especially the little ones who coughed and lay in their mothers' arms without crying, their eyes already focused on the horizon.

"Come Auntie," I said, and placed my arm under her on the other side, helping the young woman. I could feel the elder's weight heavy against my shoulder, felt my hip ache and threaten to give out. But I would not give in to the pain. I watched the soldier whose horse paced restlessly nearby, his gun level with the girl's head, his eyes on her hip, her leg. She was young enough to be my daughter. If I had my knife, I would remove this soldier's staring eyes, cut his insolent tongue from his mouth and feed it to the crows that circled overhead. I would cut the hair from his head and dance for this young girl, for her aunt, and for her husband, who was in a prison in Mankato, accused of killing a man though he was miles away. I would dance for my people, who were treated as less than animals, who were spat on and beaten. The girl's face was cut by a rock that a white woman threw as we passed through Henderson, the woman's face twisted in hate, her soul aflame in eyes that were too terrible to face, no one could look into that dark place and survive. Blood had trickled down the girl's face, but she did not flinch or wipe it from her chin. She stared at the ground, and I knew that she held herself in prayer, that as long as she prayed, nothing could move her, nothing would harm her spirit. Even when her aunt stumbled and pulled hard on her arm. The girl almost lost her balance, but with an effort that hurt me to see, she kept her slow pace, never once glancing at the soldier who rode near us. "We will make it, Auntie," she whispered. "I'm not sure where we will end, but we will get there."

We came at last to Mdo-te, to the place where the rivers meet. The long train stopped at the side of the wide river where there was a ferry waiting to take the first group of prisoners across. I felt a chill wind blow through our exhausted group, as we realized we would now be prisoners on land that is sacred to us. I looked up at the stone fort on the hill, its windows watching us like little eyes set in its walls. I could see the heads of soldiers who stood guard with their rifles. It was good they had such a large, strong army to protect themselves from these women. I spat quietly to one side, filled with disgust for such cowardly men who threatened women, who shot the ones who could not keep walking, women who closed their eyes, willing to die rather than to live any longer this way. I saw them crowd around an elder and I could not watch, I had to bury my face in my blanket. But nothing could keep the shot from ringing in my ears, from waking me at night when I dozed, too cold to sleep deeply, awakened by the rumbling in my empty stomach. I wondered where the body lay, if the woman still lay at the side of the road with no one to bury her, no one to mark her grave, no one to carry her memory forward for her family. I could not even weep for her, my tears all used for my family, and now I was dry as a bone. I was the corn husk left in the field, useless and empty.

Only my anger kept me moving, kept these two bloody feet walking, one step after another, while the girl and I held her auntie upright by the sheer force of our will. As we waited to cross the river, the girl raised her voice in a fierce ululation that took the rest of us by surprise. Another voice and then more rose as we said, "We are Dakota and we will not be defeated." But a stinging blow to the girl's head snapped it forward, cutting off her voice, so that for a moment the world around her must have turned dark. It was her auntie's strength then that held her up, kept her alive while the soldiers called harshly for silence, threatening to shoot the next woman who opened her mouth.

It was a slow ride across the river with the cold wind whipping the blankets around our legs. We could see the first few tipis already set up under the watchful eyes of the fort. This was our prison, our land reduced to this patch of woods where we would live on handouts from the government. The first few flakes of snow began to fall, softly and gently laying a white blanket on the fallen leaves. We had little food and none of our own medicines, while many of our people were already ill. Their eyes said that some had already given up, were ready to make their last journey. We looked around our frigid camp, tipis rising up ghostlike in the woods, no sign of a welcoming fire where we might warm our hands and feet at the end of this road. I wondered then if this would be the last home of the Dakota people.

Now our small group of marchers moved slowly in a long line that covered most of the bridge as we crossed to our final destination. Women walked in silence, heads bowed, weeping quietly. What a sense of hopelessness we all felt as we moved forward: grief, uncertainty about the future. We had to stop once when one of the young girls, who had been walking with her arms wrapped around her mother, simply stopped, weeping, unable to go on. Again, the other women came to her and wrapped a red scarf about her head, shielding her face from the view of the river, wrapping a blanket around her shoulders. As we approached the far end of the bridge, we could hear the ululations of some of the women who had reached the camp ahead of us. At that same moment, the sun broke through the clouds, brightening the bridge with the first rays we had seen all day, warming the hills above the river with a soft golden glow.

I walked next to Clara Strong, who told me she had just turned sixty-three and had moved back to Minneapolis from Canada. We followed the paved path from the end of the bridge that led down to the park, the original site of the prison camp. The path turned downward at a steep angle and Clara grabbed my arm while I steadied the two of us all the way to the bottom of the hill, my hip clenched in pain.

As we moved slowly downhill, we heard a solitary male voice welcome us with a traditional song, a poignant end to an exhausting journey. The singer was Art Owen, son of Amos Owen from Prairie Island, and he sang a welcome song that his aunt had recently given him. He told us later that he had not known why she had given it to him until he sang it as the marchers entered the park. He also said that when he saw the group crossing the bridge he got choked up, he felt tears on his face. "Those are the spirits," he said, pointing to his cheeks. "When you were crossing the bridge," he told the marchers, "I could see blue lights surrounding the group. Those were spirits traveling with you."

The Dakota Commemorative March crossing the Mendota Bridge,
November 13, 2002

After a ceremony dedicating a commemorative plaque to honor the original marchers, an honor dance for this group of marchers, and a feast, we were asked to gather for a closing ceremony.

When we were all seated in a large circle, Art Owen talked about the emotion of the day and the importance of the March in healing and reconciling the past. He told about his own experience on other marches—how beer bottles had been thrown at them, how people had yelled out swear words and racial epithets. He said that as long as you're in prayer, nothing can stop you. Each step you take on a march should be for a relative. When something gets in your way, you don't go around it, you go through it, otherwise it might become an obstacle next time. The feelings that came up when you were crossing the bridge were the spirits, he explained, and their presence meant that the healing had begun.

Near the end of the ceremony, Art told us how important it is to pray for each other and for our people, and to love them enough to be generous. After sharing a story about being told to leave the Capitol when he had asked that all ancestral lands be returned, he gestured toward Bob Brown, tribal chair of the Mendota Dakota, and said, "This area used to belong to the LaCroix and the James families." Art led a prayer in Dakota and ended the ceremony by leading the circle in shaking hands with each person.

When I came around the circle to Bob Brown, he shook my hand warmly and said, "Your grandmother Jenny LaCroix was my grandmother's sister." We both smiled, pleased to meet a new relative.

At the end of the evening, I was more exhausted than I have felt in my life—physically, emotionally, spiritually. But I understood, finally, that as a witness to my family's experience, and that of the Dakota people, our daily lives are only the tip of the mountain that rises above hundreds of years of generations whose experience, acknowledged or not, has everything to do with the people we become. We are the sum of those who have come before us: good, bad, wise, and indifferent. We build our lives on top of that mountain.

23 *Reconciliation*

NOVEMBER 2002
Minneapolis, Minnesota

Several weeks after the March ended, I drove my mother to the clinic on the morning of her chemotherapy treatment, the damp cold of late November chilling our bones. Despite the brisk air, my mother sat in the cold car with bare hands and neck, wearing her stylish red coat, nothing on her head. Sometimes I felt like her mother, wanting to point to my gloves, my scarf, my bulky long underwear, and tell her about the dangers of catching a chill, especially with her immune system under siege. But she has survived twenty-plus years of living with cancer without my nagging help, so I said nothing, only turned up the heat once the engine was warm. When I began to sweat, a thin layer of dew forming on my upper lip, my mother asked, "Hot flash?" with a wicked smile. I grimaced, said nothing.

As we drove, we talked about the March. "On the last day," I said, "when I saw a stake that carried the names of Louise and Narcisse Frenier, I was surprised by the deep grief I felt for what they had experienced." My mother nodded her head, understanding what I meant. It was *our* family on that original march.

My mother told me that she heard the March song, a poem I had written that Dave transformed into a haunting, poignant song that evoked the strong emotion we felt during the March. The Bird family in South Dakota had opened their studio to him, adding Sitting Bull's honor song and the drum to Dave's guitar playing, and recorded the song as a CD, which we gave to all of the marchers.

"After the first few notes," she said, "I was moved to tears. I haven't felt like that since the day you called and told me that Sue had cancer." That was the second time I had seen my mother cry—when her oldest daughter was diagnosed with ovarian cancer.

"I was choked up," she said, her words echoing Art Owen's emotion at seeing the marchers come across the Mendota Bridge. She talked about how beautiful the music was, how impressed she was at Dave's ability to combine his guitar playing with the drum. "I never paid any attention to the drums when I was growing up. I tried to forget about being Indian, about that part of my life, because people made you feel bad. But I guess you just have to accept who you are."

Hearing those words, I felt a split second of recognition, a lightning flash that signaled to me that I had been waiting to hear those words ever since she told me her story about Holy Rosary, all those many, many years ago. As if some nearly forgotten instinct knew this information should travel through the maternal line, and all of the travel and research and stories were for the sole purpose of mending the break in the line.

My mother sat staring straight ahead, lost in thought, caught by the emotion evoked by the CD.

I wanted to say to her: It was grief that you felt listening to the music, the same grief the marchers felt coming across the bridge to the prison camp in Fort Snelling. This is the grief of losing your home and your land, of feeling more shame than pride in your culture, in hearing voices call out, "Hey chief, hey Pocahontas, hey *wasichu.*" This is the grief of hunger, of holes in your shoes, of signs in windows that say "No Indians allowed." This is grief at the memory of all that was lost before you were even born, the grief of mothers and fathers who followed whatever path kept you safe, even if it meant turning away from their own blood. This is grief for the stories that were lost, the grandmothers and grandfathers who fell silent, who no longer shared their memories with their grandchildren. You weep, Mother, for the traditions that were forgotten, the old ways of honoring ancestors, of preparing traditional foods, of praying. But most of all, this grief is for you, when you came home from boarding school to find your house empty, your family gone. It's all the same, I wanted to tell her. When you weep for this music, you also weep for yourself and your family and the Dakota people, something you have never done.

But I would not say that to her, would not embarrass her with so much excess emotion. In that way, I'm like my Swedish father, all hot feelings and strong words, easy tears. Instead, I have learned to cultivate the place of silence that my mother teaches, the strength with which she moves through whatever life offers. "What can you do," she said, with a shrug of her shoulders, when told that the cancer had advanced in her body. I forced myself not to cry in her presence, not to seek her comfort when she would need my strength. "I've made my peace with it," she said. Yet she accepted the chemotherapy, determined to go on as long as she could, until she grew tired of the fight.

I thought again about the deceptively simple statement from the Ojibwe elder who said, "It's important to know as much as we can about ourselves." As we drove toward the clinic, I looked at the all-too-familiar roads we took through Golden Valley, where my parents have lived for fifty years. The new, raw suburb where we grew up without any sense of history before us had once belonged to the Dakota. They lived on the west side of Medicine Lake, near the cabin where my grandmother Maude retired. Several of the main roads—where we had learned to drive in high school, where we were driving at that very moment—were originally Indian trails that crossed the hills of the area.

Eventually, ambitious dairy farmers chopped down the forests, sold the timber to build houses for settlers, and paved the old trails. But was the past so very far away? Beneath the pavement, there remained the imprint of moccasins and the tracks of wagon wheels. They never really disappear, they simply become invisible to our eyes.

When trauma is finally acknowledged, the elders say that the healing works both back in time and forward into the future. What I had learned in trying to uncover my mother's story had bridged the rift between generations: Rosalie's life, my mother's, and mine. It had led to the March that provided reconciliation for grief and loss that had not been acknowledged in 140 years. Hearing Rosalie's story of taking refuge at Fort Ridgely rise up again, feeling the pain she must have felt in seeing family turn against family, we could learn the lessons she offered for the present. She honored the commitment she made in her marriage, but she never forgot who she was. After Louis died, Rosalie returned to the reservation with her children and lived among Dakota people until she died. It was her story that helped my mother remember who she is. With the line in our family now mending, we are all free to remember who we are. I thought of David Larsen, the historian from the Lower Sioux reservation, who said, "If you know what was taken away, then you can reclaim it."

"Just think," she said, laying her hand on the car seat between us, her wedding ring hanging loose on her finger. "This all came about because of your research into the family." Yes, I agreed, it was my nose trouble that got us into this, and we laughed.

In the doctor's office, she showed him the red bump on her arm, one of the places where the cancer has spread onto her skin. It has shrunk noticeably after her recent treatment. He nodded his head, telling her, "You've made my day." She smiled, happy, pleased that the treatment was working. Later she said, "Doesn't it feel as though things are changing for the better?"

She meant not only her improved results. I could tell that she felt caught up in the energy of the March, that she was truly part of it, just as she had always told us that she travels with us when we're away. I know that her spirit travels at night, that she dreams her way to wherever her children are, checking that they're safe, guiding them home again.

"Yes," I agreed, laying my hand for a moment on her sleeve, feeling her cool skin beneath her shirt. "I think things are changing for the better."

Family Tree

The tables on the following pages trace relationships among various members of the Wilson, Dion, LaCroix, Felix, and Frenier families. "Dion-Wilson Family" shows the generations from the author's birth family back to Rosalie LaCroix. "Frenier-Felix Family" shows the ancestry of Rosalie's daughter-in-law, Virginia "Jenny" Felix, who appears on both pages. Birth and death dates and Dakota and Ojibwe names are provided when known; not all family members are included.

Dion-Wilson Family

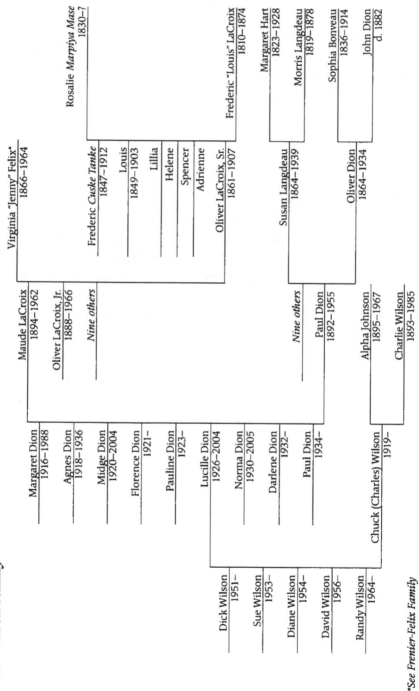

Rosalie *Marpiya Mase* 1830–?

Virginia "Jenny" Felix* 1866–1964

Frederic *Caske Tanke* 1847–1912
Louis 1849–1903
Lillia
Helene
Spencer
Adrienne

Frederic "Louis" LaCroix 1810–1874

Oliver LaCroix, Sr. 1861–1907

Margaret Hart 1823–1928

Susan Langdeau 1864–1939

Morris Langdeau 1819–1878

Sophia Bonveau 1836–1914

Oliver Dion 1864–1934

John Dion d. 1882

Maude LaCroix 1894–1962

Oliver LaCroix, Jr. 1888–1966

Nine others

Paul Dion 1892–1955

Nine others

Alpha Johnson 1895–1967

Charlie Wilson 1893–1985

Margaret Dion 1916–1988
Agnes Dion 1918–1936
Midge Dion 1920–2004
Florence Dion 1921–
Pauline Dion 1923–
Lucille Dion 1926–2004
Norma Dion 1930–2005
Darlene Dion 1932–
Paul Dion 1934–

Chuck (Charles) Wilson 1919–

Dick Wilson 1951–
Sue Wilson 1953–
Diane Wilson 1954–
David Wilson 1956–
Randy Wilson 1964–

*See Fremier-Felix Family

Frenier-Felix Family

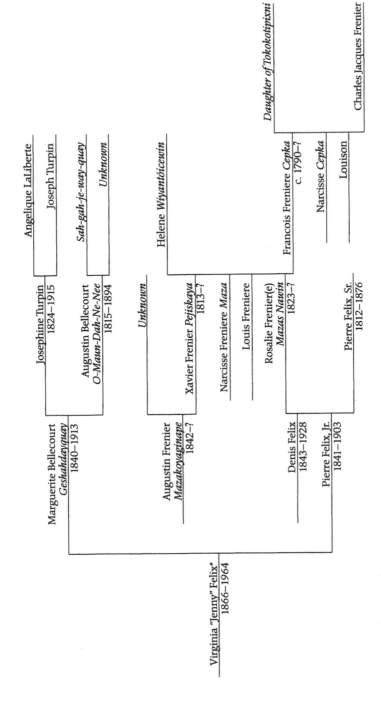

*See Dion-Wilson Family

Angelique LaLiberte

Joseph Turpin

Josephine Turpin
1824–1915

Sah-gah-je-way-quay

Unknown

Augustin Bellecourt
O-Maun-Dah-Ne-Nee
1815–1894

Marguerite Bellecourt
Geshahdayquay
1840–1913

Helene Wiyanibicewin

Unknown

Xavier Frenier Pejiskaya
1813–?

Narcisse Freniere Maza

Louis Freniere

Augustin Frenier
Mazakoyaginape
1842–?

Rosalie Frenier(e)
Mazas Nawin
1823–?

Daughter of Tokokotipixni

Francois Freniere Cepka
c. 1790–?

Narcisse Cepka

Louison

Charles Jacques Frenier

Denis Felix
1843–1928

Pierre Felix, Jr.
1841–1903

Pierre Felix, Sr.
1812–1876

Virginia "Jenny" Felix*
1866–1964

Source Notes

This section lists the sources used in each chapter, including those I relied on in creating stories. If you are interested in learning more about any of the themes or historical events that appear in these chapters, this is a good place to start.

1 *Step Back in Time*
For information about the 1862 Dakota War and the Dakota Commemorative March, see references for chapters 2, 3, and 22.

2 *Dakota War of 1862*
Information about the 1862 war and subsequent march, including dialogue that is not attributed in the text: Kenneth Carley, *The Dakota War of 1862: Minnesota's Other Civil War* (St. Paul: Minnesota Historical Society Press, 1976); Gary Clayton Anderson and Alan R. Woolworth, eds., *Through Dakota Eyes: Narrative Accounts of the Minnesota Indian War of 1862* (St. Paul: Minnesota Historical Society Press, 1988); Roy W. Meyer, *History of the Santee Sioux: United States Indian Policy on Trial* (Lincoln: University of Nebraska Press, rev. ed., 1993); interviews with staff at the Lower Sioux Agency Historic Site.

Rosalie's encounter with a frightened white woman: Helen Mar Tarble, *The Story of My Capture and Escape during the Minnesota Indian Massacre of 1862* (St. Paul: Abbott Printing Company, 1904), 16–17.

Marriage records for Frederick Louis LaCroix and Rosalie Marpiya Mase: *Early Minnesota Marriages, 1840–1854* (n.p.: n.p., 1979), 50.

Other sources for various details of the LaCroixs' life and neighbors: Franklyn Curtiss-Wedge, comp., *The History of Renville County, Min-*

nesota (Chicago: H.C. Cooper, Jr., & Co., 1916), 1:99, 100, 546, 549, 552; *Franklin* (Minn.) *Tribune,* Dec. 3, 1931; Edgar M. Bennett, "Oliver Martell: A Pioneer Gone," Dec. 29, 1904, obituary, in Dakota Conflict of 1862 Manuscript Collection, Minnesota Historical Society.

On the movement of Dakota people immediately after the Dakota War: Alan R. Woolworth, "The Displacement of Eastern Dakota by the Sioux Uprising, and Their Return," undated typescript in the possession of Alan R. Woolworth.

Information about Iron Cloud: Franklyn Curtiss-Wedge, comp., *History of Wabasha County, Minnesota* (Winona, Minn.: H.C. Cooper, Jr., & Co., 1920), 651–52, and "Dakota Portrait," in *Minnesota Free Press* (St. Peter), Mar. 10, 1858.

Reference to Samuel Hinman: George W. Crooks reminiscence, Dakota Conflict of 1862 Manuscript Collection, Minnesota Historical Society.

Freniere (Frenier) family baptismal records: Mary Hawker Bakeman, "Labors of Augustin Ravoux among the Sioux," in *Minnesota Genealogical Journal* 14 (Sept. 1995): 1317–28. More information about the family is available in Nancy and Robert Goodman, *Joseph R. Brown: Adventurer on the Minnesota Frontier, 1820–1849* (Rochester, Minn.: Lone Oak Press, 1996), 129, 146, 218, 291.

General background on fur traders: Carolyn Gilman, *Where Two Worlds Meet: The Great Lakes Fur Trade* (St. Paul: Minnesota Historical Society, 1982).

Information on family movements: Dakota Indian censuses and annuity records.

3 *The Renville Rangers*

Fred's military history: *Minnesota in the Civil and Indian Wars 1861–1865* (St. Paul: Board of Commissioners, 1890).

Sheriff Charles Roos quotation: *St. Paul Daily Press,* Aug. 22, 1862.

War information: Carley, *Dakota War of 1862;* Anderson and Woolworth, *Through Dakota Eyes* (including specific information about Augustin and Antoine Frenier, p. 140, 144, 259, 267); and Meyer, *Santee Sioux.*

Thomas Galbraith quote: Commissioner of Indian Affairs, *Annual Report,* 1863, p. 296.

Quoted information about the march moving through Henderson: Samuel Brown in *Through Dakota Eyes,* 227.

4 *Sisseton to Santee*

Williamson's quote, extensive information on Crow Creek and the Santee reservation, land allotment for both Santee and Sisseton reservations: Meyer, *Santee Sioux,* 146.

Antoine Frenier's death: Anderson and Woolworth, *Through Dakota Eyes,* 267.

Wounded Knee: Dee Brown, *Bury My Heart at Wounded Knee: An Indian History of the American West* (New York: Holt, Reinhart & Winston, 1970).

Oliver LaCroix's death: Bonnie Nordin Taylor, "Our Family History," undated narrative written by LaCroix's granddaughter on file at the Mendota Mdewakanton Dakota Community office, Mendota, Minn.

Reference to 600 children who died at Crow Creek: G. W. Knox, former Superintendent of Schools for the Winnebago Indians to Bishop Whipple, Mar. 25, 1864, Henry B. Whipple Papers, 1833–1934, Minnesota Historical Society.

Wedding announcement: *Burke* (S.D.) *Gazette,* July 2, 1915.

5 *Jousting with Windmills*

Personal recollection, family interviews.

6 *The Sixth Daughter*

St. Helena, Nebr.: http://www.casde.unl.edu/history/counties/cedar/sthelena.

7 *A Steady Paycheck*

Homestake Mining Company: "After the glitter fades," *Minneapolis Star Tribune,* Nov. 26, 2000; technical information from *History of Homestake Gold Mine, 1876 to Present* (Lead, S.D.: Homestake Mining Company, 1994).

Letter: Margaret Dion to Agnes Dion, Oct. 17, 1932.

8 *Hard Times*

Drought conditions: *Rapid Daily Journal* (Rapid City, S.D.), May-July 1936.

Agnes's death: based on interview with Pauline Dion Sandquist.

9 *A Visit Home*
Background information on Holy Rosary Mission School from *Red Cloud Indian School Centennial Memory Book* (Pine Ridge, S.D.: n.p., 1988).

Details on boarding school life: interviews with Lucille Wilson, Pauline Sandquist, Florence Buehring, and Midge Gillis.

10 *The American Dream*
Charles Abrans, *Forbidden Neighbors: A Study of Prejudice in Housing* (New York: Harper & Brothers, 1955).

11 *Leap of Faith*
Interviews with Pauline Sandquist.

12 *Starting Over*
Family information and details about Mendota: Taylor, "Our Family History."

Mendota and Pilot Knob Hill history: Bruce M. White and Alan R. Woolworth, "Pilot Knob," in *Over the Years* (Dakota County Historical Society) 45 (June 2004): 1–24.

Background on Mendota Dakota Chair Bob Brown's family: Kim Wensaut, "New Growth from Old Roots," *The Circle* (Minneapolis), Feb. 2000, including a photo of Jenny Felix LaCroix holding her youngest daughter, Marie LaCroix Nordin, mother of Bonnie Nordin Taylor.

Burial records: St. Peter and St. Paul Catholic Church, Mendota.

13 *Corn Husks & Bun Time*
Jesuit involvement in establishing boarding schools: Robert W. Galler, Jr., "A Triad of Alliances: The Roots of Holy Rosary Indian Mission," *South Dakota History* 28 (Fall 1998): 144–60; *75th Anniversary Booklet, Holy Rosary Mission, Commemorating 1888–1963* (Pine Ridge, S.D.: n.p., 1963); and Ross Enochs, *The Jesuit Mission to the Lakota Sioux: A Study of Pastoral Ministry, 1886–1945* (Kansas City, Mo.: Sheed & War, 1996).

For a different perspective on boarding schools: Tim A. Giago, Jr., *The Aboriginal Sin: Reflections on the Holy Rosary Indian Mission School (Red Cloud Indian School)* (San Francisco: Indian Historian Press, 1978); Brenda J. Child, *Boarding School Seasons: American Indian Families, 1900–1940* (Lincoln: University of Nebraska Press, 2000). Articles describing incidents of "emotional abuse, of rape and sodomy, of beatings and humiliation ... suffered at the hands of Catholic priests, nuns and other staff at Catholic Indian missions" have also appeared in *Indian Country Today* (Canastota, N.Y.) (quotation, May 12, 1993).

On boarding schools as part of assimilation policies: Frederick E. Hoxie, *A Final Promise: The Campaign to Assimilate the Indians, 1880–1920* (Lincoln: University of Nebraska Press, 1984).

Margaret Connell Szasz, *Education and the American Indian: The Road to Self-Determination, 1928–1973* (Albuquerque: University of New Mexico Press, 1974).

14 *Cowboys & Indians*
On Burke: Adeline S. Gnirk, comp., *The Saga of the Sully Flats* (Gregory, S.D.: Gregory Times-Advocate, 1978).

Pistol in the apron pocket and other anecdotal detail about family: interview with Mary Dion, Burke.

Article on Oliver Dion: undated clipping, ca. 1920s, from *Argus Leader* (Sioux Falls, S.D.) in family possession.

South Dakota geography and history: Herbert S. Schell, *History of South Dakota* (Lincoln: University of Nebraska Press, 1961).

South Dakota census records and Rosebud reservation census and annuity records, South Dakota Historical Society, Pierre.

15 *Chiefs & Scoundrels*
Homestake Mining Company: "After the glitter fades," *Minneapolis Star Tribune*, Nov. 26, 2000.

Kinship and its importance in Dakota culture: Ella Deloria, *Speaking of Indians* (1944; reprint, Lincoln: University of Nebraska Press, 1998).

Family stories of Crow Creek and Santee: Mary Myrick Hinman LaCroix, interviewed by Betty Paukert Derrick, Feb. 1980, tapes and transcript at the Minnesota Historical Society.

Article on Oliver Dion: undated clipping from *Argus Leader* (Sioux Falls, S.D.) in family possession.

Moses Stranger Horse biography: *Contemporary Sioux Painting: An Exhibition Organized by the Indian Arts and Crafts Board of the United States Department of the Interior* (Rapid City, S.D.: Tipi Shop, 1970).

16 *Indian Givers & Land Allotment*

Blood quantum and maternal descent: Mary Bakeman, ed., *The Flandreau Papers: Treasure Trove for Mixed Blood Dakota Indian Genealogy* (Roseville, Minn.: Park Genealogical Books, 1997); Robert Desjarlait, "Blood Quantum v. Lineal Descent," *The Circle* (Minneapolis), Nov. 2001.

Elements used in defining Indian identity and their evolution over time: Frances Paul Prucha, *The Great Father: The United States Government and the American Indians* (Lincoln: University of Nebraska Press, 1984).

On the infinitely complicated issue of Indian heirship: Michael L. Lawson, "The Fractionated Estate: The Problem of American Indian Heirship," *South Dakota History* 21 (Spring 1991): 1–42.

Legal status of mixed bloods: Harry H. Anderson, "The Waldron-Black Tomahawk Controversy and the Status of Mixed Bloods among the Teton Sioux," *South Dakota History* 21 (Spring 1991): 69–83.

On the Dawes Act of 1887 and land allotment policies, especially as they relate to assimilation: Hoxie, *Final Promise*; Vine Deloria, Jr., *Custer Died for Your Sins: An Indian Manifesto* (Norman: University of Oklahoma Press, 1969).

Frenier family information: Nancy and Robert Goodman, *Joseph R. Brown*.

17 *Spirit Car*

Intuition.

18 *Turning Point*

Maude Dion to Lucille Dion, 1942, exact date unknown.

19 *'Til Death Do Us Part*

Thorough discussion of intermarriage specifically as it relates to Lakota women: LaVera Rose, "*Iyeska Win:* Intermarriage and Ethnicity among the Lakota in the 19th and 20th Centuries" (master's thesis, Arizona State University, 1994). I am indebted to LaVera not only for providing a copy of her thesis but also for generously sharing her knowledge in conversations. See also Sherry L. Smith, "Beyond Princess and Squaw: Army Officers' Perceptions of Indian Women," in *The Women's West,* ed. Susan Armitage and Elizabeth Jameson (Norman: University of Oklahoma Press, 1987). For more background on the change in female roles in religion, see Vine DeLoria, Jr., *God Is Red* (New York: Grosset & Dunlap, Inc., 1973).

Some baptismal records are available in Bakeman, "Labors of Augustin Ravoux."

On the important role of fur traders and their intermarriages in Dakota culture: Sylvia van Kirk, *Many Tender Ties: Women in Fur-Trade Society, 1670–1870* (Norman: University of Oklahoma Press, 1983); Clarence A. Glasrud, ed., *L'Heritage Tranquille = The Quiet Heritage* (Moorhead, Minn.: Concordia College, 1987).

On land allotment: John D. McDermott, Jr.,"Allotment and the Sissetons: Experiments in Cultural Change, 1866–1905," *South Dakota History* 21 (Spring 1991): 43–68.

On first white children: Franklyn Curtiss-Wedge, comp., *History of Renville County*, 1292.

On the 1851 Traverse des Sioux and Mendota treaties: Anne R. Kaplan and Marilyn Ziebarth, eds., *Making Minnesota Territory, 1849–1858* (St. Paul: Minnesota Historical Society Press, 1999).

Tarble, *Story of My Capture and Escape,* 16–17.

20 *Minnesota's Legacy*
On the war: Carley, *Dakota War of 1862.*

21 *Through Dakota Eyes*
Severt Young Bear and R. D. Theisz, *Standing in the Light: A Lakota Way of Seeing* (Lincoln: University of Nebraska Press, 1994).

22 *Dakota Homecoming*
Quotations: Angela Cavender Wilson, "Voices of the Marchers," in *American Indian Quarterly* 28 (Winter/Spring 2004): 293–334.

On colonialism (suggested by Chris Mato Nunpa): Haunani-Kay Trask, *From a Native Daughter: Colonialism and Sovereignty in Hawaii* (Honolulu: University of Hawaii Press, rev. ed., 1999).

On the March: "Walking for Justice: The Dakota Commemorative March of 2002," Angela Cavender Wilson, ed., special issue of *American Indian Quarterly* 28 (Winter/Spring 2004); http://www.dakota-march. 50megs.com.

23 *Reconciliation*

On Golden Valley: Frederick W. Wandersee, *Golden Valley Remembered* (Golden Valley, Minn.: Golden Valley Historical Society, 1983); Mrs. Warner H. Lahtinen, ed., *The Golden Valley Story: 75 Years of Progress* (Golden Valley, Minn.: League of Women Voters of Golden Valley, 1962).

For information about the March song and CD, contact info@the wilsonsway.com.

Acknowledgments

Wopida tanka eciciyapi ye!

A book like this belongs, first and foremost, to the family who inspired it: my mother, Lucille Dion; her sisters Margaret, Agnes, Midge, Florence, Pauline, Norma, and Darlene; her brother Sonny; and her cousin Agnes LaCroix. My thanks to them for the grace, humor, and kindness with which they have lived their lives, and for their generosity in sharing their stories.

Special thanks to my true believers, the people who kept faith in this project through the years needed to finish it: especially my brother Dave, who shared much of this journey and his music, and my writing buddy Carolyn Holbrook. Also on this list, my editor at Borealis Books, Ann Regan, whose encouragement, insight, tough questions, meticulous attention to detail, and great humor helped make this marathon effort both life-changing and fun; and Cheri Register, my writing mentor, who gave me the perfect piece of writing advice: "Trust the process."

Thanks also to my invaluable helpers: my brothers Dick and Dave, who blazed the trail back to South Dakota; my husband Jim, for his beautiful painting on the cover and my writing studio; my dad, Chuck, who has always been ready to help; my daughter, Jodi, for her enthusiasm; my sister, Suzie, for everything; my brother Randy for his big heart; cousin Denise for her sharp eye for detail; my friend Cheryl Jaques for her unfailing support; and the old gang at the Southern for the "first" party.

All of the people on the 2002 Commemorative March have a warm place in my heart, but there are a few to whom I am especially indebted for their wisdom and generosity: Angela Cavender Wilson, Chris Mato Nunpa, Clifford Canku, Amy Lonetree, Leo Omani, Phyllis Redday, Gabrielle Tateyuskanskan, Dottie Whipple, Mary Beth Faimon, and Sharon Odegard. Thanks also to Angela and Dave Larsen for reading early manuscripts.

The list of people who helped me get started includes Kate Baker, Liz Wozniak, Carla Kjellberg, Colette Hyman, Cheryl Reed, LaVera Rose, Bruce White, Jack Broome, Mary Dion, Carol Bender, Kathleen Moore, and Ginny Martin.

My great thanks to the supportive staff at the Minnesota Historical Society, especially Debbie Miller and Alan Woolworth, who encouraged this project in its infancy. I would also like to express my appreciation to Alison Vandenberg for her energetic marketing, and of course, to Borealis Books for publishing the book so beautifully.

Joan Drury is my hero and I am in her debt as a writer. Her vision for Norcroft, a writing retreat for women on the North Shore, gave me the solitude and support to write my first story, long before I ever dreamed of a book.

The long research trips to South Dakota and Nebraska were funded by a research grant from the Minnesota Historical Society and a Travel Study grant from the Jerome Foundation.

Sadly, over the course of this project, some of the people who helped are no longer with us as this book finally reaches publication. My warmest thoughts for Willard Mackey, Chuck Robertson, Bob Brown, Norma Dion Heathcote, Midge Dion Gillis, and my mother, Lucille.